CREDO PERSPECTIVES

VOLUMES ALREADY PUBLISHED

CREDO PERSPECTIVES

PLANNED AND EDITED BY
RUTH NANDA ANSHEN

Board of Editors

W. H. AUDEN

RICHARD COURANT

MARTIN C. D'ARCY, S.J.

RENÉ DUBOS

LOREN EISELEY

WERNER HEISENBERG

FRED HOYLE

MUHAMMAD ZAFRULLA KHAN

R. M. MACIVER

F. S. C. NORTHROP

SARVEPALLI RADHAKRISHNAN

ALEXANDER SACHS

JAMES JOHNSON SWEENEY

HARRY WOLFSON

THE TORCH
OF LIFE

Continuity in
Living Experience

BY

RENÉ DUBOS

 SIMON AND SCHUSTER · NEW YORK

CARL A. RUDISILL LIBRARY
LENOIR RHYNE COLLEGE

573.2
D85x
75045
aug '71

All rights reserved
including the right of reproduction
in whole or in part in any form
Copyright © 1962 by Simon & Schuster, Inc.
Published by Simon and Schuster
Rockefeller Center, 630 Fifth Avenue
New York, New York 10020

First paperback printing, 1970

SBN 671-20469-6
Library of Congress Catalog Card Number: 62-20463
Manufactured in the United States of America

CONTENTS

CREDO PERSPECTIVES

Their Meaning and Function

Credo Perspectives suggest that twentieth-century man is living in one of the world's most challenging periods, unprecedented in history, a dynamic period when he has almost unlimited choices for good and evil. In all civilizations of the world of our modern epoch, in both socialistic and capitalistic societies, we are faced with the compelling need to understand more clearly the forces that dominate our world and to modify our attitudes and behavior accordingly. And this will only happen if our best minds are persuaded and assembled to concentrate on the nature of this new epoch in evolutionary and moral history. For we are confronted with a very basic change. Man has intervened in the evolutionary process and he must better appreciate this fact with its influence on his life and work, and then try to develop the wisdom to direct the process, to recognize the mutable and the immutable elements in his moral nature and the relationship between freedom and order.

The authors in this series declare that science now permits us to say that "objective" nature, the world which alone is "real" to us as the one in which we all, scientists included, are born, love, hate, work, reproduce and die,

vii

is the world given us by our senses and our minds—a world in which the sun crosses the sky from east to west, a world of three-dimensional space, a world of values which we, and we alone, must make. It is true that scientific knowledge about macroscopic or subatomic events may enable us to perform many acts we were unable to perform before. But it is as inhabitants of this human world that we perform them and must finally recognize that there is a certain kind of scientific "objectivity" that can lead us to know everything but to understand nothing.

The symbol of *Credo Perspectives* is the Eye of Osiris. It is the inner eye. Man sees in two ways: with his physical eyes, in an empirical sensing or *seeing* by direct observation, and also by an indirect envisaging. He possesses in addition to his two sensing eyes a single, image-making, spiritual and intellectual Eye. And it is the *in-sight* of this inner Eye that purifies and makes sacred our understanding of the nature of things; for that which was shut fast has been opened by the command of the inner Eye. And we become aware that to believe is to see.

This series is designed to present a kind of intellectual autobiography of each author, to portray the nature and meaning of his creative process and to show the relevance of his work to his feelings and aspirations. In it we hope also to reflect the influence of the work on the man and on society, and to point to the freedom, or lack of freedom, to choose and pursue one profession rather than another. For the creator in any realm must surrender himself to a passionate pursuit of his labors, guided by deep personal intimations of an as yet undiscovered reality.

Credo Perspectives hope to unlock a consciousness that at first sight may seem to be remote but is proved on acquaintance to be surprisingly immediate, since it stems from the need to reconcile the life of action with the life of contemplation, of practice with principle, of thought with feeling, of knowing with being. For the whole meaning of *self* lies within the observer, and its shadow is cast naturally on the object observed. The divorce of man from his work, the division of man into an eternal and temporal half, results in an estrangement of man from his creative source, and ultimately from his fellows and from himself.

The hope of this series is to suggest that the universe itself is a vast entity where man will be lost if it does not converge in the person; for material forces or energics, or impersonal ideals, or scientifically objectified learning are meaningless without their relevance for human life and their power to disclose, even in the dark tendencies of man's nature, a law transcending man's arbitrariness.

For the personal is a far higher category than the abstract universal. Personality itself is an emotional, not an intellectual, experience; and the greatest achievement of knowledge is to combine the personal within a larger unity, just as in the higher stages of development the parts that make up the whole acquire greater and greater independence and individuality within the context of the whole. Reality itself is the harmony which gives to the component particulars of a thing the equilibrium of the whole. And while physical observations are ordered with direct reference to the experimental conditions, we have in sensate experience to do with separate observations whose correlation can only be indicated by their belonging to the wholeness of mind.

It is the endeavor of the authors to show that man has reached a turning point in consciousness, that his relationship with his creativity demands a clarification that can widen and deepen his understanding of the nature of re-

ality. Work is made for man, not man for work. This series
hopes to demonstrate the sacramental character of work,
which is more easily achieved when the principal objects
of our attention have taken on a symbolic form that is
generally recognized and accepted; and this suggests a *law*
in the relationship of a person and his chosen discipline:
that it is valuable only when the spiritual, the creative, life
is strong enough to insist on some expression through
symbols. For no work can be based on material, technological, historical, or physical aspirations alone.

The human race is now entering upon a new phase of
evolutionary consciousness and progress, a phase in which,
impelled by the forces of evolution itself, it must converge
upon itself and convert itself into one single human organism infused by a reconciliation of knowing and being in
their inner unity and destined to make a qualitative leap
into a higher form of consciousness that would transcend
and complement individual consciousness as we know it,
or otherwise destroy itself. For the entire universe is one
vast field, potential for incarnation and achieving incan-
descence here and there of reason and spirit. And in the
whole world of *quality* with which by the nature of our
minds we necessarily make contact, we here and there
apprehend pre-eminent value. This can be achieved only
if we recognize that we are unable to focus our attention
on the particulars of a whole without diminishing our comprehension of the whole, and of course, conversely, we
can focus on the whole only by diminishing our comprehension of the particulars which constitute the whole.

The kind of knowledge afforded by mathematical physics ever since the seventeenth century has come more and
more to furnish mankind with an ideal for all knowledge.
This error about the nature of knowledge it is the hope of

this series to expose. For knowledge is a process, not a product and the results of scientific investigation do not carry with them self-evident implications. There are now, however, signs of new centers of resistance among men everywhere in almost all realms of knowledge. Many share the conviction that a deep-seated moral and philosophical reform is needed concerning our understanding of the nature of man and the nature of knowledge in relation to the work man is performing, in relation to his *credo* and his life.

Credo Perspectives constitute an endeavor to alter the prevailing conceptions, not only of the nature of knowledge and work, but also of creative achievements in general, as well as of the human agent who inquires and creates, and of the entire fabric of the culture formed by such activities. In other words, this is an endeavor to show that what we see and what we do are no more and no less than what we are.

It is the endeavor of *Credo Perspectives* to define the new reality in which the estrangement of man from his work, resulting in the self-estrangement in man's existence, is overcome. This new reality is born through the reconciliation of what a man *knows* with what a man *is*. Being itself in all its presuppositions and implications can only be understood through the totality, through wholeness. St. Paul, who, like Isaiah before him, went into the marketplace not to secularize truth but to proclaim it, taught man that the "new creation" could be explained only by conquering the daemonic cleavages, the destructive split, in soul and cosmos. And that fragmentation always destroys a unity, produces a tearing away from the source and thereby creates disunity and isolation. The fruit can never be separated from the tree. The Tree of Life can never be disjoined from the Tree of Knowledge for both have *one and the same* root. And if man allows himself to fall into isolation, if he seeks to maintain a self segregated from the totality of which he is a necessary part, if he chooses to be unrelated to the original context of all created things in which he too has his place—including his own labors— then this act of apostasy bears fruit in the demiurgical presumption of *magic,* a form of animism in which man seeks an authority of the self, placing himself above the law of the universe by attempting to separate the inseparable. He thus creates an unreal world after having destroyed or deserted the real. And in this way the method of analysis, of scientific objectivity, which is good and necessary in its right place, is endowed with a destructive power when it is allowed to usurp a place for which it is not fitted.

The naturalist principle that man is the measure of all things has been shattered more than ever in our own age by the question, "What is the measure of man?" Postmodern man is more profoundly perplexed about the nature of man than his ancestors were. He is on the verge of spiritual and moral insanity. He does not know who he is. And having lost the sense of who and what he is, he fails to grasp the meaning of his fellow man, of his vocation and of the nature and purpose of knowledge itself. For what is not understood cannot be known. And it is this cognitive faculty which is frequently abrogated by the "scientific" theory of knowledge, a theory that refuses to recognize the existence of comprehensive entities as distinct from their particulars. The central act of knowing is indeed that form of comprehension which is never absent from any process of knowing and is finally its ultimate sanction.

Science itself acknowledges as real a host of entities that cannot be described completely in materialistic or mechanistic terms, and it is this transcendence out of the domain of science into a region from which science itself can be appraised that *Credo Perspectives* hope to define. For the essence of the ebb and flow of experience, of sensations, the richness of the immediacy of directly apprehended knowledge, the metaphysical substance of what assails our being, is the very act itself of sensation and affection and therefore must escape the net of rational analysis, yet is intimately related to every cognitive act. It is this increasing intellectual climate that is calling into birth once more the compelling Socratic questions, "What is the purpose of life, the meaning of work?" "What is man?" Plato himself could give us only an indirect answer: "Man is declared to be that creature who is constantly in search of himself, a creature who at every moment of his existence must examine and scrutinize the conditions of his existence. He is a being in search of meaning."

From this it is evident that there is present in the universe a *law* applicable to all nature including man and his work. Life itself then is seen to be a creative process elaborating and maintaining *order* out of the randomness of matter, endlessly generating new and unexpected structures and properties by building up associations that qualitatively transcend their constituent parts. This is not to diminish the importance of "scientific objectivity." It is, however, to say that the mind possesses a quality that cannot be isolated or known exclusively in the sense of objective knowledge. For it consists in that elusive humanity in us, our self, that knows. It is that inarticulate awareness that includes and *comprehends* all we know. It consists in the irreducible active voice of man and is recognized only in other things, only when the circle of consciousness closes around its universe of events.

Our hope is to point to a new dimension of morality— not that of constraint and prohibition but a morality that lies as a fountainhead within the human soul, a morality of aspiration to spiritual experience. It suggests that necessity is laid upon us to infer entities that are not observed and are not observable. For an unseen universe is necessary to explain the seen. The flux is seen, but to account for its structure and its nature we infer particles of various kinds to serve as the vertices of the changing patterns, placing less emphasis on the isolated units and more on the structure and nature of relations. The process of knowing involves an immaterial becoming, an immaterial identification, and finally, knowledge itself is seen to be a dependent variable of immateriality. And somewhere along this spiritual pilgrimage man's pure observation is relinquished and gives way to the deeper experience of awe, for there can be no explanation of a phenomenon by searching for its origin but only by discerning its immanent law—this quality of transcendence that abides even in matter itself. The present situation in the world and the vast accretion of knowledge have produced a serious anxiety which may be overcome by re-evaluating the character, kinship, logic and operation of man in relation to his work. For work implies goals and intimately affects the person performing the work. Therefore the correlation and relatedness of ideas, facts and values that are in perpetual interplay could emerge from these volumes as they point to the inner synthesis and organic unity of man and his labors. For though no labor alone can enrich the person, no enrichment can be achieved without absorbing and intense labor. We then experience a unity of faith, labor and grace which prepares the mind for receiving a truth from sources over which it has no control. This is especially true since the great challenge of our age arises out of man's inventions in relation to his life.

Thus *Credo Perspectives* seek to encourage the perfection not only of man's works but also and above all the fulfillment of himself as a person. And so we now are summoned to consider not only man in the process of development as a human subject but also his influence on the object of his investigation and creation. Observation alone is interference. The naïve view that we can observe any system and predict its behavior without altering it by the very act of observation was an unjustified extrapolation from Newton's *Celestial Mechanics*. We can observe the moon or even a satellite and predict its behavior without perhaps appreciably interfering with it, but we cannot do this with an amoeba, far less with a man and still less with a society of men. It is the heart of the question of the nature of work itself. If we regard our labors as a process of shaping or forming, then the fruits of our labors play the part of a mold by which we ourselves are shaped. And this means, in the preservation of the identity of the knower and the known, that cognition and generation, that is, creation, though in different spheres, are nevertheless alike.

It is hoped that the influence of such a series may help to overcome the serious separations between function and meaning and may show that the extraordinary crisis through which the world is passing can be fruitfully met by recognizing that knowledge has not been completely dehumanized and has not totally degenerated into a mere notebook overcrowded with formulas that few are able to understand or apply.

For mankind is now engaged in composing a new theme.

Life never manifests itself in negative terms. And our hope lies in drawing from every category of work a conviction that nonmaterial values can be discovered in positive, affirmative, visible things. The estrangement between the temporal and nontemporal man is coming to an end, community is inviting communion, and a vision of the human condition more worthy of man is engendered, connecting ever more closely the creative mind with the currents of spiritual energy which breaks for us the bonds of habit and keeps us in touch with the permanence of being through our work.

And as, long ago, the Bearers of Bread were succeeded by the Bearers of Torches, so now, in the immediacies of life, it is the image of man and his vocation that can rekindle the high passion of humanity in its quest for light. Refusing to divorce work from life or love from knowledge, it is action, it is passion that enhances our being.

We live in an expanding universe and also in the moral infinite of that other universe, the universe of man. And along the whole stretched arc of this universe we may see that extreme limit of complicity where reality seems to shape itself within the work man has chosen for his realization. Work then becomes not only a way of knowledge, it becomes even more a way of life—of life in its totality. For the last end of every maker is himself.

"And the places that have been desolate for ages shall be built in thee: thou shalt raise up the foundations of generation and generation; and thou shalt be called the repairer of the fences, turning the paths into rest."*

RUTH NANDA ANSHEN

---

* Isaiah, 58:12.

THE TORCH OF LIFE:

Continuity in Living Experience

LIVING MATTER AND THE
HUMAN ANIMAL

Beast and Angel

PRIMITIVE MEN in the rain forest, like nomads in the desert, have picturesque explanations for the beginnings of the world and of life. And so have most children and adults everywhere, including the scholars in their libraries and scientists in their laboratories. Throughout the ages and all over the world, people have displayed colorful and often weird imagination in inventing theories of origin just as they have in concocting local dishes; but the theories and dishes which are satisfactory to some are unacceptable to others. For example, the ancient Chinese believed that everything in the world—life included—corresponded to different manners of association between two opposite principles. In their philosophy, the yin symbolized the dark, moist, cold, feminine principle, and the yang its bright, dry, warm, masculine counterpart.

The expressions yin and yang are not very meaningful to me, but I have learned to be tolerant of them because I make even less sense of the mathematical symbols which my colleagues, the theoretical physicists, now employ to describe the physical world. I realize of course that modern physics appears to give a factual picture of reality because atomic power developed out of the cabalistic symbols $E=mc^2$; but I find it equally remarkable that the

Chinese have built out of yin and yang a philosophy which has served them well for two thousand years. Interestingly enough, modern physicists frequently use words which the ancient Chinese would have liked. They contrast matter with antimatter, and many of them claim that the idea of "complementarity" is essential for understanding the cosmos.

Complementarity, as I understand the word, denotes the logical relation between two concepts which appear mutually exclusive, both of which, nevertheless, have to be used in order to achieve a complete description of reality. For example, some optical phenomena can best be described by regarding light as a wave, and others by regarding it as a corpuscle—even though waves and corpuscles seem to have nothing in common in ordinary experience.

My only justification for mentioning Chinese philosophy and theoretical physics, two topics of which I am ignorant, is that they provide some kind of excuse for the fact that I have built the thesis of the present book out of what appear to be contradictory arguments. In reality, however, I have tried to present complementary rather than contradictory aspects of life and of human nature. Just as Cervantes depicted man in the form of both the earth-bound Sancho Panza and the errant knight Don Quixote; just as Robert Louis Stevenson made the same person be at times Dr. Jekyll and at times Mr. Hyde, so I have attempted to present with equal favor two opposite pictures of reality, both of which I regard as simultaneously valid and equally useful.

I do not claim that these pictures express deep philosophical truth; only that they correspond to the dual manner in which all human beings—philosophers and scientists as well as laymen—perceive reality when they experience it in the flesh instead of discussing it in the abstract. Whatever theoretical views men hold of creation, they behave in practice as if they believed that life is different from matter, and human consciousness different from other forms of life. It is from this pragmatic point of view that I shall consider living processes and human behavior in all the manifestations which constitute the living experience of sensitive and rational men.

From experimental science I have learned that everything in the world is inexorably determined by natural laws; yet I am on the side of the moralists who proclaim that normal man is entirely responsible for his actions. I know that all living organisms, including men, are physicochemical machines, and that the more we learn of biological structure and function, the better we understand life; but I believe also that every time a particular man, a particular dog, or a particular amoeba acts or refuses to act, something occurs which could not have been entirely predicted from physicochemical knowledge. I know that even the most learned, sentimental, and idealistic human being is but an evolutionary product originating from inanimate matter; but I believe also that man is an arrow pointing the way to some spiritual goal of evolution. I know that human behavior is conditioned by the past, by everything in the environment, even by the smallest speck of dust and the most distant star; but I believe, nevertheless, that it is the privilege of man to exercise free will; indeed, to act consciously in a manner that will affect future events. Finally, I have every reason to think that the most common determinants of human behavior are today, as they always have been, crude material appetites and selfish ambitions; but even the most ordinary events of life lead me to believe that the performance of mankind is far more exciting and inspiring than could ever have been expected from the trivial and selfish motivation of the apelike creatures which constitute the human species.

It is this extraordinary contrast between the meanness

of man and the greatness of his deeds, that I should like
to consider first in the following pages. To introduce the
subject I might explore what Goethe had in mind when
he wrote in *Faust* that Mephistopheles was the "power
that aims for evil, but nevertheless does good." Instead, I
shall turn to a more commonplace experience, one that
can be recaptured by any visitor to New York City. This
experience is perhaps the more meaningful to me because,
as an immigrant from Europe, I still sense today, after so
many years, that it was from the very rawness and crudeness of the American continent that mankind created the
dreams of freedom and of unlimited possibilities still
identified today with the New World.

The traveler approaching New York City from the
ocean first perceives Manhattan as an ethereal mass slowly
emerging from the water. He long remains unaware of
the confusing and overpowering mass of steel and of
stone, and he can imagine a luminescent spirit ascending
into the sky. The illusion creates different moods, depending upon the weather and the hour of the day. At times
the island seems to float mysteriously in clouds or in the
mist, as if it were some holy mountain in an ancient Chinese scroll; often it shimmers in precious pinks and blues
like one of William Blake's visions come to life; at dusk
or at night it glows like a flaming torch. Never does it
evoke only brute force and material wealth.

The spiritual quality of the spectacle makes one forget
the crudeness of its material origin. Yet these rising towers which so deceptively reflect the splendors of heaven
are, in fact, bound to hard bedrock and are built of harsh
materials; they represent wealth and arrogance. Each and
every one of the tall buildings is the product of materialistic urges and was erected not as a contribution to a
concerted common task, but as a display of power and
pride. How did it happen that this uncoordinated effort,
motivated by ruthless ambition, could have engendered

so spiritual a silhouette against the sky? Through what mysterious alchemy did the random interactions of gross individual strivings bring into existence, in the course of half a century, one of the most unexpected and grandiose architectural symphonies of the world? The Manhattan skyline thus symbolizes a very perplexing aspect of human life—the fact that mankind can convert crude appetites into the splendors of civilization, and transmute greed into spirituality. Throughout historical times, man has created better than he planned and than he knew. Works of lasting value have often emerged from efforts aimed at the satisfaction of immediate and material urges.

Entering Manhattan by the Brooklyn Bridge also contributes to this schizophrenic view of mankind. Both sides of the bridge are crowded with tense human beings, aggressive and often cruel, bent on extracting money from each other, and obsessed with the pursuit of gross sensual pleasures. As judged from their behavior, most of them appear unaware of the sky; they seem undisturbed by the brutality of the noise, by the harshness of the artificial lights, by the uncouthness of the environment in which they function. Automobiles, trucks, and electric trains generate on the pavement of the bridge a deafening vibration, creating a metallic kind of hell in which men seem condemned to move mechanically and endlessly. But the bridge itself is like a gigantic diaphanous web stretched across the sky, indeed like a lyre on the strings of which light plays at all hours of the day and of the night, singing the poesy of industrial civilization.

The massive pillars of the Brooklyn Bridge evoke ancient temples in which profound mysteries were once enacted. This illusion seems to become reality at night, when Manhattan sparkles and vibrates through millions of illuminated windows, each one of them a symbol of man's passionate struggle for power and for creation. And there comes to mind the memory of J. A. Roebling, the

architect of the bridge who died from a wound con-
tracted during the first stages of the construction, and his
son Washington Roebling who continued the task. Washington Roebling's health broke under the crushing load of
responsibilities, but, though paralyzed, he continued to
supervise the work from his bedroom window. The Roeb-
lings' lives, thus dedicated to the construction of this
poetical masterpiece of steel and stone, show man at his
highest—more concerned with worthy creation than with
health and comfort.

It is clear that the most profoundly different attributes
still coexist today in all men, as well as in their works—
from greed and cruelty to asceticism and self-sacrifice, from
natural earthiness to the highest aspirations, from materialistic achievements to spiritual ecstasy. This pluralistic
character of human nature makes the science of man
much more complex than the sciences concerned with
matter or with other living things, and it poses to sociol-
ogy and to human medicine problems vastly different from
those of veterinary medicine and of general biology.

The strange fact is that, while the design of the human
machine clearly reflects an animal origin, and while human behavior is still largely determined by animal appetites, nevertheless, the most interesting and significant aspects of man's life are derived from traits which do not
exist or are barely noticeable outside of mankind. I might
be permitted to relate a recent personal experience which
helps to convey, by concrete image, how the humanness
of man has set him apart from the rest of creation, and
has thus given rise to scientific problems different from
those of the orthodox natural sciences.

The experience took place in the public park of a large
eastern city at lunch time during the month of May. A
lovely breeze, blowing from the Great Lakes, had brought
a mass of warm dry air, with a luminous sky—one of
those days when New York and Boston remember that

they are at the latitude of Naples and Rome. The park
was animated by all kinds of men and women, young and
old, shabbily or well dressed. Some of them ate their
sandwiches with lively gestures and conversation; others
sprawled on the grass exposing to the sun as much of
their bodies as was decently permissible; still others
walked hand in hand in an amorous mood. There were
many pigeons in the park, also eating, also strutting
about, the males displaying their plumage in courtship
around the females. As I watched this pleasant spectacle,
the similarity in the type of behavior exhibited by the human beings and by the pigeons seemed to make it obvious
that man was nothing but an animal—or, at best, a creature who had learned to refine somewhat the attributes
and also the physical pleasures inherited from his evolutionary past. For a while, I settled comfortably in the
orthodox scientific concept that human nature can be understood from an analysis of the chemical components of
which the body is built—the hemoglobin of the blood, the
proteins of the muscles, the lipids of the brain, and the
nucleic acids of the genes. I also played with the notion
that the mind can be described in exact mechanical terms,
because it is in some ways like an electronic computer,
only more complicated, more entertaining, and also more
appealing than an IBM machine.

Walking away from the park in the afternoon, my attention was caught by an inscription on the wall of a
church in a nearby street. The inscription marked the
hundredth anniversary of the birth of the Hindu poet
Rabindranath Tagore, with a quotation from one of his
books. "I believe in a spiritual world," Tagore stated, "not
as something separated from this world, but as its most
real innermost truth." And these words brought back to
mind that not only in India, but all over the world, there
are innumerable human beings for whom problems of the
spirit are more important than satisfactions of the body.

Because the beautiful spring day made me so acutely
aware of sensuous appetites and pleasures, I was almost
embarrassed to remember that, in the Catholic world, the
month of May is dedicated to the Virgin Mary, an en-
dearing symbol of love and of so many other human attitudes which transcend completely the sensuous aspects of
life. Clearly, the spiritual aspects of human nature are
just as much a part of reality as are the bodily structures
and the animal appetites. Ever since man has emerged
from his brutish origin, the beast and the angel have co-
existed in him.

The Science of the Body and Mind

BY SEPARATING the animal and the spiritual
aspects of human nature, I have brought to the surface
one of the most controversial subjects of science and philosophy, the concept of body-mind dualism. Is it really
true, as I seem to have implied, that the body and the
mind are two distinct entities? Or are they merely two
different manifestations of the integrated structures which
make a living organism? There is at present no conclusive
evidence to decide between these two alternatives so fundamentally different one from the other. However, I must
acknowledge that I find the second hypothesis more con-
genial than the first, and indeed that what we express by
the word mind is, in my opinion, a manner of response by
the living organism to the total environment—a response
which is more or less elaborate, depending upon the complexity of the organism and perhaps even more upon its
history. According to this view, mind is not something peculiar to man; to varying degrees, it is manifest in all
living things. Clearly, however, mind corresponds to a
characteristic which is much more elaborate in man than
in the rest of creation, because man has a richer and

more subtle perception of the cosmos, and because he responds to a much wider range of stimuli. Consciously and unconsciously, he is linked to cosmic influences which include not only the present, but also what he remembers of the past, and the manner in which he visualizes the future. The origin of these unique qualities of human nature is very obscure, but what is certain is that man does not feel isolated as a freak in nature. The teaching that it is a duty to respect all forms of life is more than a sentimental dictum. It expresses man's awareness that there exists some profound unity among all living things, that they all possess some quality which sets them apart from inanimate matter.

Whatever the theoretical views one may hold concerning body-mind dualism, the fact is that every man behaves in practice as if he believed that the body and the mind are two separate entities. Even those who regard mind as but a manifestation of the body machine, nevertheless find it useful to deal with it as if it could be considered apart from the body. Interestingly enough, this peculiar "as if" behavior is especially evident among scientists. Even the most materialistic among them take it for granted that the study of man, as well as of other living things, involves two very different kinds of activities. The functions of the body and its structure are studied in the scientific laboratory and so are the appetites, needs, instincts, and biological drives of all living things including man. In contrast, the mind and its creations are considered the province of psychologists, theologians, philosophers, and artists. It must be recognized, however, that this attitude, which is almost universal at the present time, is rather new. In fact, it did not become crystallized until the seventeenth century, when the French scientist and philosopher René Descartes gave the blessing of philosophy to the doctrine of body-mind dualism in his book *Discours sur la Méthode.*

Descartes taught that the body is a machine and therefore can be studied as such by the ordinary techniques of natural sciences. In contrast, he regarded the human mind as an immaterial and supernatural principle, linked to the body of course, but through a kind of union that God had intended to remain beyond human understanding. Descartes' enormous and lasting influence is probably responsible for the fact that, while the body became a legitimate subject of scientific analysis in the Western world, those aspects of human life which are identified with the mind have been greatly neglected by experimental scientists. The growth of modern biology and of medicine is the expression of the tremendous advances in the knowledge of the body machine which have resulted from the mechanistic scientific attitude symbolized by Descartes. But unfortunately, this same attitude has tended to make scientists shy of analyzing consciousness, thereby greatly narrowing the scope of scientific studies devoted to the phenomena of life. Since biologists regard living organisms as so many machines, they neglect the phenomena not found in machines which are precisely those peculiar to life. Descartes' influence has been particularly disastrous in the study of man, because it has discouraged scientific study of those aspects of human nature which do not fit well in the orthodox body-machine concept.

All experimental scientists know, of course, that science cannot answer such broad and ill-defined questions as "What is the true nature of life?" or "What is the total nature of man?" The genius of experimental science is to formulate other questions more limited in scope and more precise in wording, for which answers can be obtained by observation or by experiment. Science proceeds step by step, not trying to solve at one stroke large philosophical problems, but contributing information relevant to their understanding. The moot question is whether it is possible to apply this method to questions which bear on the properties peculiar to life and to the mental attributes which separate man from the rest of creation.

For many hundreds of years scientists have studied in great detail the aspects of man's body and behavior which make him resemble animals. More recently they have focused attention on the structures and phenomena which are common not only to men and animals but also to all other forms of life, including plants and microbes. At present they emphasize more and more those aspects of all living things which can be described through the knowledge of inanimate chemical substances. One need not be a scientist to appreciate the phenomenal success which has attended this approach. By progressively shifting emphasis from man to simpler living things, and then from life to matter, science has proved beyond doubt that there are common denominators in all the things that we know—the structure of a bone or of a stone; the sparkle in the eyes of a child or the light emitted by a firefly.

On the other hand, it is clear to everyone that even the most primitive microbe has properties which no longer exist when it is dead and which are never found in a pure chemical substance, however complicated it may be. Everyone knows also that even the least civilized man has several mental attributes which are not found in the most intelligent ape or porpoise. In view of these facts, scientists might find it profitable to reverse, now and then, the direction of their inquiries and to emphasize not the similarities but the differences between life and matter, between man and animals. Such a reversal would not imply a denial of the scientific attitude as already noted; scientists would formulate limited questions to be answered by experiments, and let the results and findings suggest other experiments that would sharpen and enlarge the meaning of the differences observed. Science always proceeds through questions which, progressively, become more and more subtle, and there is no reason a priori why this approach cannot be just as successful for the recognition of the differences that exist between life and matter, as it has been for the demonstration of the similarities between them.

From what is presently known, Homo sapiens—the modern form of man—has existed on earth for approximately a hundred thousand years in numbers large enough to constitute a population. Barring catastrophic accidents, it can be expected that man will continue living on earth for many millions of years. Using a somewhat fanciful kind of arithmetic, it can be calculated from these figures that the present age of humanity corresponds to very early childhood in the life of a human being. Pursuing still further the same farfetched comparison, reading and writing were invented a year ago; Plato, the Parthenon, Christ, date from but a few months; experimental science is just a few weeks old, and electricity a few days; mankind will not reach puberty for another hundred thousand years. In this perspective, it is natural that so far mankind should have been chiefly concerned with becoming aware of the world of matter, listening to fairy tales, and fighting for pleasure or out of anger. The meaning of life, the problems of man and of society, become dominant preoccupations only later during development. As mankind outgrows childhood, the proper use of science may come to be not only to store food, build mechanical toys, and record allegories, myths, and fairy tales, but to understand, as well as possible, the nature of life and of man in order to give more meaning and value to human existence.

From Material Body to Spiritual Body

PAUL THE APOSTLE symbolically expressed in his first letter to the Corinthians a truth about human

nature which each generation of biologists has restated
in the words of its contemporary scientific knowledge:
"The first man is of the earth, earthly: the second man
is . . . from heaven. . . . It is sown an animal body; it is
raised a spiritual body." These statements are as true in
the light of evolutionary knowledge as they are in the
light of Paul's faith. For us, however, the problem is to
understand how modern man has remained rooted in the
material nature from which he originated, and of which
he is still a part, yet has so long continued his ascent
into his paradoxical humanity.

Since known facts are not sufficient to account for the
apparently dual nature of man, faith in various forms
has rushed in to fill the vacuum and to satisfy the longing for some form of answer. Most commonly, faith
takes the form of religious dogma, tracing to an omnipotent God the creation from inanimate matter of life and
of man, with all their attributes. In contrast to orthodox
religious faith, the scientific approach is to ascertain objective and verifiable facts, whether or not these facts
explain the origin of life and of man. Science has shown
in great detail that all living forms share many characteristics in common and are therefore interrelated. It has
obtained what seems convincing evidence that they are
all derived one from the other; indeed, that there exists
a continuous chain of intermediate forms linking man
to the most primitive microbe. All scientists believe that,
throughout its long evolution, the human species has
been subjected to the same natural laws which rule over
the rest of the cosmos. The most spiritual aspects of the
human condition obey immutable laws, just as do the
crudest constituents of inanimate matter of which man is
made, and in which he lives. Science tries to discover these
laws and to unravel the forces and the mechanisms which,
in the words of Paul, raised the material body into a
spiritual body.

One of the greatest advances made by the human mind has been to demonstrate the falsity of the ancient fear that events and actions originate from the whims of capricious and irrational deities. It is obvious, however, that we know very little of the actual order prevailing in creation, that most occurrences remain as yet unexplained, even those of everyday life. Each and every human being lives in expectation, and often in dread, of events that he cannot foresee, and that he usually does not understand after they have happened. Yet, belief in the existence of a rational order persists because it satisfies the human mind, and also because there are many situations in which this belief permits useful action. Rational science thus leads to a form of faith which, to paraphrase Kant's words, is not sufficient for complete understanding but is, nevertheless, adequate for effective behavior.

In reality, religious faith and scientific faith are rarely in serious conflict at the present time in the Western world. All scientists realize that their knowledge is so grossly incomplete that they cannot hope to explain everything. On the other hand, the most enlightened among religious persons not only conceive of God as omnipotent and omniscient but also believe that the mind of man has developed a rational system which is compatible with His laws. They take it for granted, in fact, that the cosmic order recognized by Science is His order. There still exists, of course, a conceptual gap between religious faith and the scientific attitude with regard to origins, but the painful conflicts of the past century have been replaced by a state of tolerance and of peaceful coexistence.

The most profound and troublesome conflict, it seems to me, is not between religious and scientific faiths, but between these two forms of faith and the problems posed by belief in the existence of free will. It is, of course, very difficult to explain how living things could possibly have the freedom to choose and to act, if one believes that they have been created by an omnipotent and omniscient God; but the same difficulty exists if one believes them to be the products of natural forces that determine what they are today from what they have been in the past and from the influences that impinge upon them. Although the problem applies to all living things, it is, of course, especially puzzling in the case of man. Theologians, philosophers, and scientists have dealt with questions of free will in many ingenious ways in an attempt to reconcile biological freedom of action with the strictures imposed by divine ordinance or by scientific determinism, but the very profound differences that still exist between the various explanations proposed so far make it clear that the problem is not near being solved. I bring it up here not to discuss it in philosophical terms, but because it underlines one aspect of the human condition which gives to human life its peculiar character.

Whatever their convictions—religious, philosophical, or scientific—human beings behave as if they did, in fact, believe that they can exercise free will. What is more, they behave as if this was also true of the larger animals. Individual persons differ in the vigor with which they try to control the course of their lives, but no human being is the completely passive victim of his destiny. It would not be helpful to elaborate on this statement, since no explanation or illustration would be as convincing as one's own experience. Nevertheless, the words of a celebrated scientist may help to carry the point home: "One's ability to move his hand at will," the American physicist Arthur Compton stated a few years ago, "is more directly and certainly known than are Newton's laws. If these laws deny one's ability to move his hand at will, the preferable conclusion is that Newton's laws require modification."

It is obvious, in any case, that belief in determinism, whether it be based on religious or on scientific reasons, does not engender a passive attitude among its adherents.

Calvinists, just like Marxists or materialistic scientists, proclaim in the abstract that everything is determined by God's will or by antecedent causes, but in practice they act as if they believed in the effective power of free will. It seems justified therefore to accept as a paradoxical but real fact, that while living things must obey the laws of nature, nevertheless they behave as if they possessed some freedom in their decision to act and in their choice of action. Man is higher than the amoeba or than the dog on the scale of life because he is endowed by nature with a wider range of freedom.

Human life is concerned to such a large extent with facts which do not have a material existence, that scientific knowledge often seems to have little relevance to the problems most important for mankind. A point of view widely held today was well expressed by Samuel Johnson two centuries ago: "The truth is that knowledge of external nature, and the sciences which that knowledge requires or includes, are not the great or the frequent business of the human mind . . . we are perpetually moralists, but we are geometricians only by chance."

It must be admitted that modern scientists feel most at ease when they shun the problems which interest the moralist, and when they limit their attention to the properties of the physical world and to the material basis of life. True enough, they also attempt to study the behavior, and to some extent the history of living things, particularly of human beings; but this type of knowledge is considered by many as marginal to science, indeed, as not genuine science. This, however, is a rather new attitude, as shown by the fact that, until a few centuries ago, many scientists considered themselves philosophers and moralists.

It would be out of place to discuss here the reasons which lead so many modern scientists to rule out of their professional thoughts and activities the very facts which are the most interesting and important aspects of human life—namely, the concern with the past, the commitment to spiritual values, the eagerness to project the present into the future. But it is worth noting that this intellectual shyness of the scientific community with regard to the problems peculiar to man probably accounts, in large part, for the lack of interest in science among the general public. In his professional operations, the scientist has become almost exclusively interested in the *mechanisms* of the phenomena that he studies, and therefore in their immediate causes. But human beings are, as a rule, more vitally interested in the "wherefore" than in the "why," and this is also true of scientists themselves when they function outside of their own professional specialty. The main reason for which men desire to know whence they came, and how they are what they are, is that they would so much like to know whither they are going. Concern about the future is the most powerful motivation of man, and we shall see in subsequent chapters that it also plays a role, still mysterious but nevertheless very real in the development of all other living things.

Whereas it is very difficult to arouse public interest in the static, descriptive, and analytical aspects of science, the popular response is likely to be rapid and intense when the subject of discussion deals with the dynamic aspects of creation and of life. The emotional involvement would become even greater if science would find it possible to consider within its province the study of man not merely as a machine or as one animal among so many others, but as a sensitive, imaginative, and ethical being who remembers the past, and who lives emotionally in the future. Scientists can study man only if they are willing to recognize, not only in the abstract but as an objective fact, that his behavior is determined by historical factors and by nonmaterialistic, "unnatural" goals.

Purpose and Adventure

IN THIS BOOK, I shall emphasize the attributes which differentiate living phenomena from matter and man from animals. My discussion will be based in part on orthodox scientific facts, but also on another kind of facts which seem to me just as real and objective, yet are usually not considered scientific because they cannot be measured or described with precision. Although it may be intellectually dangerous to mix measurable facts with a less well-defined kind of knowledge, I believe that this approach is necessary at the present time for dealing scientifically with problems of life and of the humanness of man. Without it, scientists will discover more and more of the physicochemical laws that govern the mechanical operations of living things, but they will leave out of consideration the creativeness of life and the values of man.

I realize that much of what I shall say will be subjective, coming from the marrow of my bones rather than from rational and organized knowledge, and it is to emphasize subjective aspects of my discussion that I began the book with an account of personal responses to the Manhattan skyline, to the Brooklyn Bridge, and to human life seen from a park bench. This approach was also dictated by another reason which is more difficult to express but far more important. It has to do with the manner in which we apprehend and try to understand the very spirit of life and of the human adventure.

The products of life commonly exhibit an impressive degree of organization and of beauty, as if they were the results of thoughtful effort. And yet there is no evidence whatever that the snail is aware of the architecture of its shell, the butterfly of the design on its wings, the rose of the delicacy of its petals. Similarly, the works of mankind often achieve great aesthetic beauty or intellectual

grandeur, even though they were not planned with this
end in mind—as if they were the product of an unconscious process. This occurred in our era for the Manhattan
skyline, as it did a few centuries ago for the silhouette of
medieval European villages clustered on a hillside and
crowned with a church steeple. Many of the most sophisticated scientific theories also seem to have emerged more
or less spontaneously, having begun as rather naïve concepts and from very simple observations, and acquiring
a classical structure of logic only at the end of their evolution. In an arresting image, Arthur Koestler has spoken
of the seventeenth-century pioneers of modern science—
for example, J. Kepler and Galileo Galilei—as "sleep-
walkers," because they could not possibly have had a
clear conscious vision of the distant goals toward which
they were moving, and which are being reached only now.
There is no doubt indeed that many—if not all—of the
great achievements of mankind originate from visionary
perceptions, unanalytical and vague, and that it is only
after they have achieved maturity that one can define and
describe the forces which have influenced their course.

In her *Patterns of Culture,* Ruth Benedict emphasized
that the great cultures of the past developed as by a kind
of organic growth which was not determined by a conscious choice, or by clear formulation of purpose: "It is
the same process by which a style in art comes into being
and persists. Gothic architecture, beginning in what was
hardly more than a preference for altitude and light,
became by the operation of some canon of taste that developed within its technique, the unique and homogeneous
art of the thirteenth century. It discarded elements that
were incongruous, modified others to its purposes, and
invented others that accorded with its taste. When we
describe its process historically, we inevitably use animistic
forms of expression as if there were choice and purpose
in the growth of this great art form. But this is due to

the difficulty in our language forms. *There was no con-scious choice, and no purpose.* What was at first no more than a slight bias in local forms and techniques expressed itself more and more forcibly, integrated itself in more and more definite standards, and eventuated in Gothic art. What has happened in the great art-styles happens also in cultures as a whole. All the miscellaneous behaviour directed towards getting a living, mating, warring, and wor-shipping the gods, is made over into consistent patterns in accordance with unconscious canons of choice that de-velop within the culture."

What Ruth Benedict said of cultures and of art forms holds for many other human creations. But while it is a fact that unconscious forces have molded historical events and will continue to influence human destiny, it is also true that as more is learned of these forces, what was once unconscious progressively becomes conscious. There is also reason to believe that even though an action is un-conscious, this does not mean that it is accidental, or irrational. The human intellect is but an expression of thought patterns which have evolved in direct associa-tion with nature, and for this reason it reflects the pat-terns of nature. Most of its manifestations are still mysterious because they have not yet been recognized and analyzed. But there is nothing mystical in this mystery, only incomplete knowledge. To a very large extent, the advance of civilization is determined by the ability to replace unconscious processes by conscious operations. This is the deep role of philosophy and of science in human history.

However, what is still so completely mysterious as to acquire for many human beings a mystical quality, is that life should have emerged from matter, and that mankind should have ever started on the road which so clearly is taking it further and further away from its brutish origins, and differentiating it more and more completely from the

rest of creation. It is the urge for adventure and for understanding, the desire to achieve some noble work, which
constitutes the essence of the human condition. Whatever his faith in this matter—religious or scientific—every
thinking and sensitive man hears in his heart an echo of
the words that Tennyson attributes to Ulysses, urging his
companions to "sail beyond the sunset."

> *There lies the port; the vessel puffs her sail;*
> *There gloom the dark, broad seas. My mariners,*
> *Death closes all; but something ere the end,*
> *Some work of noble note, may yet be done.*

THE QUALITIES OF LIFE

The Emergence of Life

IT WOULD BE helpful to start this chapter
with a definition of life and with a description of the first
living forms. Unfortunately, these matters raise questions
to which there is as yet no answer and which are so
charged with emotion that they foster dogmatic attitudes,
as much among agnostic positivists as among orthodox
church members.

While it seems at first sight easy to tell a living thing
from an inanimate object, in reality the differences between life and nonlife become more and more tenuous
as one turns attention from animals and plants to the
smallest known organisms—in particular to the submicroscopic viruses. Many viruses have been obtained in a
pure chemical state as if they were inert substances, and
yet have been found to retain in this form the property
to reproduce their kind and thereby to cause disease
as if they were living things. Several kinds of viruses occur
naturally as beautiful crystals which can be recognized
with the electron microscope and which have properties
resembling those of nonliving molecules of similar dimen-
sions, except for the fact that they increase in numbers
when inoculated into the proper kind of plant or animal.
The crystalline state of these infective particles poses a

problem which bears not only on the nature of viruses, but also on the nature of life. Is there a well-defined, critical property—or set of properties—which differentiates life from nonlife; or is it impossible to delimit sharply inanimate matter from living organisms because there exists a continuous spectrum of intermediate forms between them? Unfortunately, neither scientists nor philosophers can yet agree on the criteria that would define the ultimate essence of Life.

I shall take the position that Life is not at all understood as an abstract concept, and that it is known only as an experience. In this respect, the biologist finds himself in an intellectual situation not unlike that of the physicist who studies gravitational forces. The physicist does not understand the ultimate essence of gravitation; what he observes and measures are the effects of gravitational force on objects under various conditions. Similarly, what the biologist studies is not Life as a principle but only the structures and functions of living things, and also their responses to various stimuli and in various circumstances.

Although no one can define life, many are those who have strong convictions concerning its origin. In reality, however, these convictions are based on prejudice and speculation rather than on factual knowledge. The difficulty of proving any theory of the origin of life is revealed by the fact that there exists, in this regard, as much deviation from scientific orthodoxy as from religious orthodoxy. The problem of origin does not exist, of course, for those who adhere strictly to any one of the orthodox religious creeds; for them, the solution consists simply in accepting to the letter the teaching of the Book of Genesis that God created all living forms. However, many Jews and Christians now believe that the story of creation is symbolic rather than descriptive and that the meaning of the symbol has not yet been entirely deciphered. The seven

days of Genesis correspond in their view to the eons of
the cosmic evolutionary scale. Indeed, an increasing number of religious persons now look to scientific knowledge
for a more meaningful interpretation of the symbolic
account of origin. Like physicists who accept the existence
of gravitation as a fundamental force of nature without
claiming to understand what it is, many Jews and Christians
are willing to wait for further information before attempting to give a scientific interpretation of the phenomena
peculiar to *Life*.

At the present time, it is the scientific community which
provides the most lively forum for the expression of con-
flicting views concerning the nature and origin of life.
Whatever their religious faith or lack of it, all scientists
agree on the fact that the various living forms are interrelated, and that man also is part of the immense web
which unites animals, plants, and microbes in the fabric
of life. But beyond this point, there are many shades of
scientific opinion on the subject with little prospect, at
present, for the emergence of a unified scientific dogma.

The most strongly entrenched and articulate sect—
which one might call a scientific orthodoxy—holds to the
belief that there does not exist any fundamental difference
between the inanimate and the living world, and that life
is just a more complicated expression of matter. Early in
the history of the globe, according to this view, matter
became organized through a series of accidents into forms
capable of self-reproduction by duplication—and thus it
acquired one of the essential properties of life, namely,
the power to replicate itself. This happened a very long
time ago, since the earliest traces of life so far detected
are those of algae found in rocks which are estimated to
be approximately two thousand million years old! These
algae being complicated organisms, it can be assumed
that they had been preceded by simpler forms, and it is
certain therefore that the origin of life is more ancient.

How ancient cannot be determined because the first forms of life have certainly disappeared without leaving any detectable trace. It is assumed that the initial step in the transformation of matter into living things consisted of a change which endowed some substance with the property of reproducing itself. This substance, which became "living" by this initial accident, then evolved through chemical action and became transformed into all the living forms that we know today. At each step, Darwinian selection of the forms best fitted to a given environment would have provided the guidance for adaptive evolutionary transformations.

The bearers of hereditary characteristics, which are transmitted by each organism to its descendants, contain a peculiar class of substances known as nucleic acids. These substances, which are the chief constituents of the genes, have the further remarkable property of being able to undergo now and then accidental changes—called mutations—which thereby alter the hereditary endowment of the organism of which they are a part. Thus, in the light of present knowledge, gene nucleic acids seem to be the most characteristic and most essential constituents of living things as we know them. Indeed, there is an increasing tendency among scientists to identify them with Life as a principle. This attitude has been recently summarized as follows by Asimov, an exponent of orthodox scientific knowledge, in his book *The Intelligent Man's Guide to Modern Science*. Asimov states that "the key step" in the emergence of living forms was "the formation through chance combination of nucleic acid molecules capable of inducing replication. That moment marked the beginning of life." Accepting this dogmatic statement at its face value, it follows that, still in Asimov's words, "modern science has all but wiped out the border line between life and non-life."

The theory identifying the origin of life with the first

formation of gene nucleic acids gives the illusion of being factual and objective, because it is expressed in words which refer to substances and to operations which are familiar to laboratory workers. It has indeed the virtue of concreteness and of corresponding to a kind of precise knowledge, which can be stated in chemical formulae. Its precision stands in sharp contrast to the fuzzy descriptions and explanations of theologians, philosophers, and old-fashioned naturalists. In reality, however, there is no valid evidence that the preceding account has anything to do with the *origin* of life. No one has shown, so far, that one could generate new life in the laboratory by synthesizing nucleic acids, or any other substance. At best, all statements concerning the origin of living things are working hypotheses, based on assumptions with but a flimsy theoretical basis, and which have never been subjected to experimental verification. It would be out of place, of course, to discuss these assumptions here, but it may be useful to illustrate by a few examples how wide is the gap which separates the views held by different scientists, each one of them an eminent expert in his own field, concerning the nature and the origin of life.

At one extreme is the opinion expressed by the chemists Stanley L. Miller and Harold C. Urey that only six major chemical problems remain to be solved before one can understand the origin of life. All these problems have to do with the laboratory synthesis of nucleic acids and of proteins; their solution is within the range of existing knowledge. Once these problems are solved, according to Miller and Urey, it will be possible to visualize through imagination how the first living form originated, and also to synthesize another one in the laboratory.

There are many other scientists, however, who think that nucleic acids are so complicated in structure that they are not likely to have been the first kind of molecules to be capable of self-reproduction. In other words, these substances, far from being at the origin of life, would instead constitute late products of its evolution. As brought out in an international congress held in Moscow in 1958, there could have been produced under the conditions of primitive atmosphere, a wide range of substances similar to those now found in living things, and some of these substances might have been the original replicating molecule. Furthermore, substances used for one purpose in primitive organisms find a different application in other organisms as evolution proceeds. In view of these facts, it seems unwise to make dogmatic statements as to what kind of substances were first involved in living processes. It seems rather foolhardy to extrapolate from present-day biochemical structures to the primitive state of affairs.

There is, furthermore, something rather fuzzy in the very concept of "origin" of life. It is commonly assumed that the momentous event by which a living thing first originated from organic matter was but one step of the orderly process of cosmic evolution which led from matter to life and from life to human consciousness. What we *know* of evolution applies only to things already living, and this cannot be used as evidence for explaining the passage from inanimate matter to life. In some recent papers, the celebrated geneticist Theodosius Dobzhansky made the tantalizing statements that "evolution *transcended* itself when it achieved this momentous step"; and, elsewhere, that "in producing life, cosmic evolution overcame its own bounds; in giving rise to man, biological evolution *transcended* itself" (italics mine). These statements might be interpreted to imply that the change from matter to life constituted a very unusual event, and that something rather mysterious happened when cosmic evolution "*transcended* itself" to produce a substance that had, in potential, the properties of life, including the ability of man to admire a cloud and to imagine God. Yet other evolutionists suggest that there may not be anything very unusual, after all, in the emergence of a living molecule, that it has happened several times in different places in the cosmos and may still be happening today. These newly emerged living molecules would not now survive on the earth because they would be immediately devoured by existing forms of life.

During recent years, a few scientists have been bold enough to revive the ancient theory that life might not, after all, have originated from matter in the simple crude way that chemists and geneticists propound with such assurance. At the end of an article published as recently as 1960 in the English journal "New Scientist," W. T. Asbury made the startling statement that the universe "is a unity, self-consistent, ever expanding, ever creating, the same everywhere else and there are no 'accidental' phenomena, *probably not even life.*" More explicitly, the physicist Niels Bohr also suggested that "the very existence of life *must be considered an elementary fact,* just as in atomic physics the existence of a quantum of action has to be taken as a basic fact that cannot be derived from ordinary mechanical physics" (italics mine). In one form or another, the concept that life entails the operation of some principle of nature which is as yet ill defined seems to be gaining ground at the present time; and there is reason to believe that it is the fear of entrenched scientific orthodoxy which stills the voice of many who believe that life involves something more subtle than the latest chemical formulae for nucleic acids.

The outsider, watching the conflict of attitudes among scientists regarding the nature and origin of life, probably gains the impression that science is a House Divided, where hopeless confusion reigns. The truth, however, is very different. There exists, in reality, an enormous area of agreement among scientists of all shades of opinion, and the differences of interpretation apply only to the

advancing edge of knowledge where facts are still scant
or uncertain. The formulation of a useful working hypothesis is an essential part of the scientific process, because it helps to determine what kind of questions to ask,
the type of phenomena most likely to be worth investigat-
ing, and how to design experiments. Hypotheses are like
trial balloons which reveal the comparative strength and
direction of the various currents of knowledge and thought.
Divine creation, the operation of a natural force as yet
unknown, and direct emergence from matter, are the three
balloons which today carry men's thoughts on the origin
of life. All three are vulnerable, and the information that
they bring will be useful in the future only to help develop
more sophisticated techniques of exploration.

Life and Matter

THE WORK OF THE past hundred years has
established, beyond doubt, that all living things—whatever their size and whether they be men, animals, plants,
or microbes—possess many physicochemical characteristics in common. In particular, all of them depend upon
the same fundamental reactions for their supply of energy;
all synthesize proteins of approximately the same amino
acid composition for structural purposes and for enzy-
matic activity; and all transfer their hereditary endowment
from cell to cell through the agency of submicroscopic
particles consisting largely of nucleic acids. These physicochemical similarities provide, of course, spectacular con-
firmatory evidence for the theory of evolution. They
greatly increase the likelihood that all living forms studied
so far have something common in their origin, that they
may indeed all derive from a single point of genesis and
have progressively differentiated only in secondary characters. But granted that all forms of life exhibit great

chemical similarities, at least two very different working hypotheses can be considered to account for this remarkable unity. One is that the same forces which operate in the inanimate world also act on ordinary matter in such a way as to produce the characters of life; the other is that some unknown principle runs like a continuous thread through all living forms and governs the organization and operation of their physicochemical characteristics.

The first theory is supported by the well-established fact that all living phenomena always go hand in hand with definable reactions which occur according to physicochemical laws identical with those which operate in the inanimate world. This fundamental fact makes it possible to study the living body as if it were an ordinary machine. Indeed, there is no doubt that many of the greatest advances in modern biology, and its applications to medicine, have grown directly out of this theoretical concept.

The proponents of the second hypothesis acknowledge, of course, that all biological phenomena obey known physicochemical laws, but they point out that this fact is not sufficient evidence to prove that life is merely an expression of these laws. Correlation and lack of contradiction with the phenomena of physics and chemistry could be compatible with other theories of life. Furthermore, it appears, at first sight at least, that living processes exhibit many characteristics which are not found in the inanimate world, and there is ground for the assumption that these involve the operation of some directive force as yet unidentified. Such a belief does not imply that living phenomena are outside the rule of natural laws, but rather that science has failed so far to recognize the forces peculiar to the living world, probably because it has focused its attention on the material world.

As appears from this cursory and oversimplified statement, there is one essential question at the basis of all the theoretical arguments concerning the nature of life. The question is to determine whether it is truly a fact that some of the characteristics of living things do not have their counterpart in the nonliving world. It would be useless and unwise to try to guess the answer to this question from the very meager knowledge available at the present time. There are reasons to believe, furthermore, that the problem will be very difficult to formulate in terms of experimental operations and, thus, cannot be solved very soon. What is possible and useful, however, is to try to recognize the properties which are possessed by all living things, and which disappear from them as soon as their life ceases. This can be done objectively, irrespective of one's prejudiced view concerning the origin of life and its essential nature. To describe life as experience manifested through the observable behavior of living things is far less ambitious than attempting to define its ultimate nature. True enough, this humble effort is not likely to provide a philosophical answer to the riddle of existence, but it will certainly help man to learn more of the biological basis of his own nature, and this in turn will help in formulating, with greater wisdom, a social and ethical philosophy of human life.

Change and Persistence

THE MOST STRIKING PROPERTY of living things is, of course, that they are potentially capable of reproducing their kind—of replicating themselves, as is the expression. This power of replication exists at all levels of complexity in the living world. A microbe which divides and multiplies produces similar microbes, just as an oak produces acorns which grow into similar oaks, and just as a dog begets dogs, and man begets human beings. We have already mentioned that this power of replication operates through a mechanism which is essentially identical in all living things, and which probably resides in nucleic acids organized in structures called genes. Although the marvelous knowledge concerning these bearers and transmitters of hereditary characteristics is very recent, it has been presented in popular writings so often and so well, that it need not be further elaborated here. But there is need to emphasize that genes are but one part of the living cell and are no more able by themselves to insure growth and reproduction than are the other parts. Granted the astounding properties of the genetic hereditary apparatus, they are not sufficient to account for the phenomena of replication.

The fact is that the living organism begins its life, not as an assembly of genes, but as an organized cell. The gene nucleic acids do not have to manufacture, at the start, all the complex structures and substances on which life depends. These are present in the living organism at the time of division. The task of the genes, therefore, appears far more modest than what is usually claimed. It consists of giving a limited number of instructions to a system which is already poised to function. An analogy can be made here with the operations of an electronic computer. As stated by the English biologist Beament, "The set of instructions fed into the computer by e.g. punched cards, sets into motion a sequence of events in which the structure of the computer plays an essential part. The way it is wired and the nature of its parts represents a considerable amount of information which the punched cards need not and do not supply. The genes, as catalysts, act precisely like a punched card instruction."

It is clear, in brief, that the genes, wonderful as they may be as isolated structures, are ineffective by themselves. More generally, the same thing can be said of all the other constituents of the organism. Life is possible only when all these constituents operate together and in accordance with a certain pattern of reactions; nothing simpler than an entire living cell is capable of self-duplication. Thus we recognize here, at this very threshold of life, a principle which holds true at all levels of life, up to the most evolved types of social organization. All the parts of a living system are interdependent. There is not one structure, one reaction, or one process, which alone can define life. As we know it through experience, in contrast to what we surmise from the analytical study of lifeless parts, life manifests itself only in the form of complex structures in which a host of mutually dependent processes are integrated according to an orderly and unique pattern.

In addition to the ability to replicate themselves, living things exhibit the power to undergo certain changes. As we have seen, some of these modifications have their seat in the genetic apparatus, and thus are lasting and transmitted to the descendants of the organisms. Other changes are more transient and occur only as a response of the organism to a given situation; they are not hereditary, and they progressively disappear when the original stimulus is eliminated. The ability to change exists in all organisms—from viruses to man; and it applies to an enormous range of body structures and functions, perhaps to all of them. Nothing comparable exists in the nonliving world.

It is this ability to undergo changes—both hereditary and transient—which makes it possible for living things to become adapted to so many different situations. Man is particularly well endowed in this respect, and the adaptive changes of which he is potentially capable have enabled him to colonize the earth. A few examples will suffice to illustrate the range of mechanisms and of organic structures which are involved in these changes.

The shape of the body and the pigmentation of the skin, which affect so profoundly the ability of man to function and survive under certain climatic circumstances,

are determined to a large extent by the hereditary constitution; these hereditary characteristics originate directly
from the gene nucleic acids. In contrast, the antibodies
which protect against infection are not inherited; they are
produced by certain tissue cells only as a response to the
presence of the proper microbes, or to a vaccine made
from microbial constituents and products. The callusing
of the skin is another kind of change which results from
an adaptive reaction to trauma; in this case adaption
occurs at the organ level, just as an increase in muscle
development follows physical exercise. Skills and memories can be regarded as adaptive changes involving the
individual as a whole; and at a still higher level of organization, languages and customs are manifestations of responses by the social group.

It is apparent, therefore, that the ability to undergo
changes is found at all levels of life and affects all activities of living things. In fact, change is even more meaningful in the case of man than it is in the case of primitive
forms of life. A fully developed human being cannot be
thought of as an isolated creature. His potential attributes
become fully realized only when he functions within a
social matrix, on which he depends, against which he
reacts, and to which he contributes. From microbe to
human society, life is an expression of the mutual interdependence of parts.

Thus, the ability to change is a fundamental characteristic of life. But to be compatible with the continuance
of life, any change must become harmoniously integrated
with the various structures and functions that the organism
has inherited from its evolutionary past. Life is historical,
and it can continue only if the new becomes part of the
old, or, at least, does not conflict too violently with the
established order. One of the characteristics of life is that
the past survives in the present and determines the accept-
ability of any change, just as the future determines its
viability.

Purpose and Life

THERE IS another aspect of life which does not seem to have its exact counterpart in the inanimate world. Throughout the development of any organism, the morphological and functional changes *anticipate* the future functional and morphological requirements of the fully developed organism and of its progeny. Everything in the egg is prepared before hatching for the needs of the chick.

Some of the most spectacular examples of biological foresight are provided by the social insects. William Morton Wheeler, who devoted much of his life to the study of ants, pointed out that social organization has started, quite independently, in at least twenty-two different groups of insects. In each case, the basis is a continuing association between parent and offspring; the young stay with the female parent or with both parents, forming a cooperating group in which different individuals develop traits which fit them for a special function. In the termites, ants, wasps, and bees this simple idea of parent-young association has developed tremendous complexities, predetermined in the genetic make-up of the insect.

The extraordinary specialization and integration of insect societies—with their queens specialized for reproduction, their workers and soldiers specialized for different kinds of work and of warfare—has excited the wonder of all those who have observed them in detail, an excitement which Maurice Maeterlinck's *The Life of the Bee* conveyed to the lay public a generation ago. It must be acknowledged, however, that there is, as yet, no adequate explanation for the unselfishness—if this word can be used here—which is so much in evidence in colonies of bees, ants, or termites. The nearest approach to some understanding of the problem is provided, perhaps, by recent observations on the structure of their brain. In all animals,

the brain can be divided into two sections, one corresponding to the segmental part of the psyche—selfish and predictable—and the other to the suprasegmental, which
transcends the immediate and the selfish. Interestingly
enough, it happens that the top ganglion of the brain—
the suprasegmental—is larger in social species of insects
than in solitary forms. The unselfish care of the young
in all animal species is controlled from the cerebrum, an
organ which might be regarded as the biological seat of
cooperation.

To state that these wonderful arrangements are the outcome of evolution is a descriptive account of what has
happened but provides no understanding of how and
why. The same query applies to the development of the
various organs of the body, each so precisely specialized
for a particular function. It is useful to remember that the
original meaning of the word "organ" is "working tool."
This derivation is not an accident. It symbolizes the fact
that an organ cannot be completely understood only from
a description of its structure; the knowledge of how it is
made must be supplemented by the experience of what
it can do. The organ acquires its full signficance only when
it functions, and when its performance is integrated in the
life of the organism not only in the present, but for the
future.

The assertion that the organism develops as if it has
some awareness of its future is a statement fraught with
three thousand years of argument about the meaning of
life and its direction. At one pole is the faith identified
with the Aristotelian doctrine that life cannot be described
only in terms of its elements and origins, because it involves preordained goals; knowledge of the ends of an
organism, of its wherefore, would then be essential for its
understanding. At the other pole is the view of those who
hold that there is no goal, only haphazard events. According to this theory, the emergence of any structure or func-

tion would be the product of mutational accidents, and its persistence would be determined by the further accident that it happens to fit or not to fit in the environmental niche where the organism happens to fall. In the words of George Gaylord Simpson, one of the most thoughtful and learned American students of evolution: "Organisms diversify into literally millions of species, then the vast majority of those species perish and other millions take their place for an aeon until they, too, are replaced. Species evolve exactly as if they were adapting as best they could to a changing world, and not at all as if they were moving toward a set goal."

Whatever one's faith in this controversy—which apparently has lasted as long as men have given thought to the problem of the meaning of life—it is certain that in practice the searching for the purpose of an organ, or a function, is at least as likely to contribute to its understanding as is the study of its mechanism or of the cause from which it originates. The simple reason for this fact is that any character, old or new, is not likely to survive long unless it serves a useful purpose. It must be functional under the normal conditions of competitive life—even though the scientist often has difficulty in recognizing the usefulness of the function.

Surprisingly enough, physicists—who deal with the world of matter—seem to have been intellectually more receptive to the implications of this fact than are biologists—who are assumed to be concerned professionally with the world of life. In this regard, it is entertaining to contrast with the words of the biologist G. G. Simpson, quoted above, some statements recently made by the Danish theoretical physicist Leon Rosenfeld: "It is practically impossible, even with the most perfect knowledge of all the laws of physics and chemistry, to predict what kind of organism will result from a given structure of such complexity. We must realize that in order to get complete understanding of organisms we need the concept of function. *We must somehow know beforehand what the function of a certain organ is in order to be able to understand its structure.* We here meet with another type of causality, functional causality, which is obviously complementary to the ordinary causality of physics and chemistry, from which this concept is absent" (italics mine). Thus, according to this physicist, the intimate study of *living* things (as contrasted with the detailed analysis of lifeless fragments derived from them) may yet provide evidence for a kind of natural principle which has not been revealed by the study of matter, even of the matter of which living things are made.

The Creativeness of Life

NOT ONLY IS IT impossible to really understand a structure apart from its role in the whole organism, but in addition, there exist in living things creative potentialities that become manifest only under special conditions. On the one hand creativeness can originate from mutational changes in the genetic mechanisms. These genetic changes make possible biological innovations which survive in the modified forms of life, if other circumstances permit.

The creativeness of life, however, does not come only from these accidental changes in the genetic apparatus. It can also manifest itself through the association between independent living organisms which display unforeseeable new properties when they function together. These creative associations constitute an aspect of life which has hardly been studied, which indeed is ignored by most biologists. Although well-authenticated examples abound, only a very few can be mentioned here as illustrations.

One might begin with the case of the plants and insects which cannot fully develop unless they carry in their tissues the proper kinds of microbes, living in constant and intimate association with them. The microbes supply their hosts with essential foodstuffs that the latter could not obtain otherwise; and, furthermore, their presence acts as a sort of stimulating and regulating mechanism which permits the development of structures and functions not realized in their absence. Thus, some species of tropical plants remain stunted and undifferentiated, if they do not contain peculiar kinds of microbes which stimulate the production of nodules on their leaves. Some of the most beautiful orchids cannot develop from seed unless in association with the right kind of fungus. Lice and roaches are among the many species of insects which have been shown to depend for growth and survival upon association with microbes.

One knows of very extraordinary associations between certain animals and luminescent bacteria. Under the proper conditions these microbes produce a steady luminescence, but the luminescence can be made to appear intermittent by secondary controlling mechanisms operated by the host animal. In the crustaeceans *Coeloryhnaes* and *Hymenocephaleus,* the brightness of the bacterial luminescence can be increased or decreased by the movement of pigmented materials that the animal produces; in *Photoblepharon,* the light emission is controlled by the screenlike movement of the eyelid and in *Anamolops* by rotating the organ which carries the luminescent bacteria in a closed pocket so as to conceal them at the proper time.

Very recent studies have revealed that the decorative value of many plants is determined by the fact that they live in association with certain viruses. In tulips and larkspur these viruses determine beautiful designs and color variegations in the petals of the flower. In the white-veined honeysuckle or the flowering maple (Abutilon), they enhance the decorative value of the plant by affecting the distribution of the chlorophyll, thus causing patterns of green and white in the leaves.

A well-known illustration of the creativeness of biological associations is provided by the fact that plants of the legume family—such as clover, alfalfa, peas, beans, lentils, or sweet peas—normally live in association with particular kinds of bacteria which remain localized in nodules on the rootlets. These nodule bacteria fix the nitrogen of the air and thus contribute to the nutrition of the legume plant. They also stimulate the production in the root of a red pigment almost identical with the hemoglobin of human blood, which neither the plant nor the bacteria can produce when living in the absence of the other.

Even more striking is the case of the lichens, organisms which had long been thought to represent a special group of lowly plants with many species and varieties. Lichens occur in many intriguing forms and in a wide range of colors, on the bark of trees, on rocks, and in wastelands. One of their characteristics is their ability to become established and to prosper under the most inimical conditions, even in places where life appears impossible. What makes lichens important for our discussion is that they are not ordinary plants, as had been assumed. In reality, they are made up of two different kinds of micro-organisms living in intimate associations. Each lichen is the symbiotic outcome of one particular species of alga and one particular species of fungus, the two micro-organisms being so intimately interwoven that it is extremely difficult to separate them.

There is no doubt that the alga and the fungus supplement each other nutritionally, when they are associated in the form of lichen. Furthermore, their symbiosis often results in other effects of far greater biological interest. Thus, lichens exhibit complex morphological structures and synthesize peculiar organic acids, aromatic substances (such as *mousse de chêne*) and pigments (such as litmus), that neither the alga nor the fungus can produce when living alone. Looking at the delicately shaped and bright red structures of the common lichen known as "British Soldier," it is difficult to believe that such startling appearances can result from the associations of a microscopic alga and a microscopic fungus, both of them inconspicuous. Nor would it have been possible to predict from the known characters of its two components that the lichen could synthesize the peculiar chemical substances that it produces, or exhibit such great ability to survive heat, cold, or dryness.

Thus, it is clear that symbiosis in lichens is more than an additive association. It illustrates an attribute of life which has never been adequately studied by experiment, nor indeed reproduced, namely, the *creative* force of association between two different types of organisms which results in the production of unpredictable new structures, functions, and properties.

Examples of biological associations resulting in the emergence of new properties could be cited *ad infinitum*. In fact, they are so varied and occur so widely among all kinds of living things, even among the smallest in size and the simplest in structure, that there is reason to wonder if living things ever exist in nature except in association with others. It may well turn out that the creativeness of life depends in large part, perhaps entirely, upon the ability of individual organisms to form with others, intimate associations which generate new structures and properties. As we shall see later, this concept also applies to man, whose spiritual development is the outcome of highly integrated social relationships.

Teleology and Telenomy

THE PROPERTIES common to all living things —such as the ability to reproduce themselves, to undergo changes which fuse the past and the future in the present, and to create novelty out of existing structures—are the expression of one general character which seems to constitute a very profound difference between life and inanimate matter. According to one of the most fundamental laws of physics, the universal tendency in the world of matter is for everything to run downhill, to fall to the lowest possible level of tension, with constant loss of potential energy and of organization. In contrast, life constantly creates and maintains order out of the randomness of matter. To apprehend the deep significance of this fact one need only think what happens to any living organism —the very smallest as well as the largest and most evolved —when finally it dies.

As long as the organism lives it takes raw matter from its environment, builds it up and organizes it into patterns which are immensely complex but constant for each species. Life results in the creation and maintenance of order, against all odds, in opposition to the destructive forces of the universe. Then, at the very moment of death, the beautiful organization of the living individual begins to break down. The ordered arrangement of patterns soon disintegrates into a jumble of molecules which progressively fall to lower and lower levels of organization and of complexity, until picked up again by another living organism which creates out of them a new kind of order.

It is obvious, of course, that the pattern of organization is, to a very large extent, preordained for each type of organism. In fact, the pattern exists in the sperm and in the egg before conception, just as it does in the most lowly microbe before division. The same kind of hay can become the substance of a rabbit, or cow, or bacillus— even though after the death of the rabbit, the cow, or the bacillus their constituents once more progressively disintegrate and return to a common state. While these facts are matters of common observation and have long been known, they constitute, nevertheless, one of the deepest mysteries of life.

As was the case for the question of origin of life, ignorance of the forces which determine the preordained pattern of an organism encourages the formulation of intellectual and emotional attitudes not supported by adequate evidence, and these attitudes not infrequently evolve into convictions. Stated broadly, all the different views on this subject are variants of two opposite doctrines. One is that the future of any living organism is inherent in the organism itself, that there is some thing that pulls it onward from in front. According to this view, each one of the activities of the organism is defined by its end, rather than by its past; it involves some aim and purpose. This philosophical concept, commonly referred to as teleology, is at present in bad repute among most scientists. The orthodox view is that the design characteristic of each type of organism, is the expression of accidental mutational changes which have become successfully integrated in the organism during the course of its evolutionary history. Natural selection would be the ordering principle here. It would operate blindly, pushing life onward from behind and bringing about organization, more or less automatically, without conscious purpose or any awareness of an aim.

As just mentioned, teleology is now in bad repute among orthodox scientists. But although they repudiate the word, most of them still resort extensively to teleological thinking in their work. In most research on problems of life, the usual course is to observe interesting phenomena that appear somewhat mysterious and unexpected, and then to try to find the "why" of these phenomena. This attitude implies, of course, a belief in some kind of purpose, and, in fact, most investigators base their work on the hypothesis that important structures and functions do, in some way, play a useful role in the life of the organism. Teleology, it is often said, is like an attractive woman of easy virtue, without whom a biologist cannot function happily, but with whom he does not want to be seen in public. Recently, a number of thoughtful biologists have tried to escape from this embarrassing situation by urging that the word teleology be abandoned altogether and replaced by the new word telenomy. All biologists realize that a word is needed to denote the fact that most structures and functions are valuable for the ultimate ends of the organism. But, whereas the word teleology is tainted with overtones of preordained design, its substitute, telenomy, would imply that blind natural selection has been responsible for what appears at first sight to be manifestations of purpose. The situation here recalls the attitude of Calvinists, Marxists, and positivistic scientists who, as pointed out in the first chapter, believe in absolute determinism, but, nevertheless, behave as if they believed in free will. Likewise, the most violent opponents of teleology constantly use it in their scientific work, even when they call it by another name.

It is a remarkable fact that whatever the views individual biologists hold concerning the origin of living things, and irrespective of whether they believe in the old-fashioned teleology or in the more sophisticated telenomy, there exists among them a large body of agreement concerning the qualities of life. As we know it today, life operates as if most of its structures and functions were designed to fulfill some ultimate end, for the good of the individual and of the progeny. Life has its roots in the past, and its activities are projected into the future. Furthermore, it is a creative process, elaborating and maintaining order out of the randomness of matter, endlessly generating new and unexpected structures and properties by undergoing spontaneous changes, and by building up associations which qualitatively transcend their constituent parts. Clearly then, living things cannot be differ-

entiated from the inanimate world only in terms of structures and properties. Their unique characteristic resides
in the fact that their behavior is determined by their past
and conditioned by the future, a property as yet mysterious but real nevertheless.

It is important at this point to emphasize once more that
the preceding statements do not correspond to an abstract definition of the ultimate essence of life. They refer
only to its manifestations as experienced in living things.
When applied to man, they suggest that he is the most
advanced expression of life to the extent that his awareness and his activities are more intensely concerned with
his memories and his goals. The fact that life cannot be
defined, only experienced, is a great lesson in humility
and should discourage any dogmatic statement as to its
origin and its ends. Because the mind abhors a vacuum,
most of us find it necessary to accept a faith or make
hypotheses, but we should remember that certitude—scientific and philosophical, as well as religious—is, to a
large extent, an expression of intellectual conceit and always deceptive. As Francis Bacon wrote 350 years ago,
"The universe is not to be narrowed down to the limits
of the Understanding,—but the Understanding must be
stretched and enlarged to take in the image of the Universe as it is discovered."

COSMIC CYCLES AND
BIOLOGICAL PROGRESS

The Myth of Eternal Return

EVEN THE PESSIMIST who feels that the world is out of joint and that the worst is yet to come, nevertheless believes that mankind could, if it so wanted, achieve health, prosperity, and happiness. We take it for granted that there exists a one-way road from our brutish past to the Golden Age of the Future. Crooked and dangerous as the course of the road to this Golden Future may be, we regard the possibility of progress as self-evident, limited only by our willingness to make the necessary efforts and to accept the guidance of knowledge and wisdom. In reality, however, the very idea of progress is far from evident and universal. Indeed, belief in progress represents such a recent attitude, that, according to historians, the idea did not become widespread until the eighteenth century.

It is obvious that men who live close to nature—as did most men until not so long ago—have little occasion to experience continuous progress toward something new and better. What impresses them, rather, is the recurrence of the old, the endless repetition of similar events. Ecclesiastes had good reason to lament more than two thousand years ago that "there is nothing new under the sun"—either in the ways of nature or in the ways of men. Every day the sun rises and sets; every month the moon displays its regular phases; every year the seasons come and go, bringing in their train a more or less predictable order of changes in the weather, in the vegetation, in animal life, and in human moods. Social phenomena also exhibit a distressing predictability. Civilizations are born, flourish, and decay; hope follows despair; good and evil seem forever to compete and to engage in a tug of war on the stage of the human comedy.

This endless recurrence of natural events, and these monotonous repetitions in the human drama, so profoundly influenced the primitive mind that they shaped many of its beliefs and practices. All people in the past became emotionally involved in the natural cycles, and they marked the turning points in recurrent phenomena by religious festivals and rites, most of which persist even today. The most obvious, of course, are the pagan celebrations in all parts of the world to mark the reawakening of life in the spring, and the gathering of crops in the fall—celebrations which have become so deeply integrated in human life that they still stir deep currents in the blood of modern city-dwellers. Just as the sap starts flowing in the trees, and the birds begin nesting when the sun becomes warmer, so do men and women experience the need to expand their increased vital energy—either in the form of Mardi gras, of pole dances, or of marriage ceremonies. And everywhere in the fall, harvest festivals mark the ripening of the grain, of the pumpkin, and of the grapes.

Very early in the human epic, earlier perhaps than the emergence of festivities dedicated to food and to the animal senses, the rhythms of nature inspired celebrations of a more abstract quality. The worship of the sun at a special moment of the year was practiced among the Chaldeans and the Natchez in much the same way as it had been in prehistoric times at Stonehenge and Carnac. The solar events also inspired some of the most cherished and beautiful myths of the ancient Mediterranean world. Daphne, the dawn, sprang from the waters at the first blush of morning light; then, as the tints of early day faded gradually in the light of the rising orb, she fled from Apollo who tried to win her.

The death of nature in the winter and its rebirth in the spring gave rise to many legends. Frazer shows in *The Golden Bough* that the cult of Astarte and Adonis originated far back in neolithic times and had to do with agricultural magic. Adonis, the youthful masculine god, was loved by Astarte. In spite of her forebodings, he went off to hunt and was killed by a wild boar. He was mourned and lamented by the goddess who eventually secured his release from the underworld. This legend inspired elaborate ceremonies in ancient Greece. The marriage of the god and goddess was sometimes ritually enacted by a sacred couple, sometimes symbolized by sexual union between worshipers at the annual festival in early summer. A sacred dirge was sung by women with bared breasts to commemorate the god's death, and his effigy was thrown into water. Little gardens of seedlings in pots were set out, to sprout and wither in memory of his youthful vigor and premature death, and were then thrown into vivifying water to symbolize the hope of his resurrection the next year. Scarlet anemones, symbolizing the blood from his fatal wounds, were strewn upon his image.

Astarte was a form of the mother-goddess, symbolizing the fertility of nature. Adonis was the masculine principle needed to fertilize the feminine element as well as the crop which withers in autumn but grows again in spring. His death represented the human sacrifice which was originally made to insure the crop's rebirth, the ritual of the sexes expressed fertility magic, and the sacred lament for the god was part of the rite for securing his resurrection.

Another entrancing legend was that of Persephone, daughter of Demeter, the goddess of vegetation. Persephone was raped by Hades who kept her underground for three months every year, and during that period all vegetation became quiescent. The whole cycle of the yearly change and the sprouting of the grain, symbolized in the Persephone myth, were celebrated every spring in Greece by the Eleusinian ritual. Hyacinthus also symbolized alternating decay and return to life in nature.

There is no doubt that the many legends, processions, mysteries, and sacrifices which ruled ancient life according to the regular pattern of natural events, imposed upon the human mind the concept that the world repeated itself, endlessly, from year to year. The awareness of this eternal return is still, of course, a powerful force among us. Witness the vigor of the New Year tradition when every person, except the most disenchanted, entertains for a few moments the illusion that once more everything starts anew.

As shown by Mircea Eliade in *Cosmos and History*, the myth of eternal return has had a profound significance in the development of human thought. Ancient man generally believed that there are cycles in social history, just as there are recurrent phenomena in nature. There were Golden Ages in ancient times, and there will be Golden Ages in the future; the trials of the moment are but the winter months between the times of plenty. Ancient man could not conceive of endless progress, because he believed that history must repeat itself indefinitely.

The Torch of Life

THE DEEP REALITY of the endless cycle between life and matter is made evident to the senses by looking at the earth, handling it, smelling it, and observing its changes from season to season. After death, plants and animals fall to the ground; there they rot and putrefy; and in the process they are transmuted into the humus of the soil out of which new life is produced. Under a thousand symbols, men of all religions and philosophies have sung and portrayed this repeated return of living things to inanimate matter, and the ever-repeated emergence of new life. There is, indeed, a fascination and perhaps truth in the ancient creed that life is always arising anew from matter, as Aphrodite came out of the foam of the sea. Men have also long believed that living things are endowed with a special kind of force—in itself eternal—capable after death of entering into all sorts of new, diverse combinations to re-create life. In the ancient Latin world these problems found their most passionate expression in Lucretius' poem "De Rerum Natura."

Untiringly, Lucretius reiterated in his poem that nothing arises save by the death of something else, that Nature remains always young and whole in spite of death at work everywhere; that all the living forms that we observe about us are but so many passing forms of a permanent substance; that all things come from dust, and to dust return—but a dust eternally fertile. "What came from earth goes back into the earth," Lucretius wrote. "What was sent down from the ethereal vault is readmitted to the precincts of heaven. Death does not put an end to things by annihilating the component particles; it only breaks up their conjunction. Then it links them in new combination." Or elsewhere: "Whatever earth contributes to feed the growth of others is restored to it. The universal mother is also the common grave. . . . Sea and river and springs are perennially replenished, and the flow of fluid is unending."

There is, indeed, scientific truth and philosophical depth, as well as poetic beauty, in the famous lines of

Lucretius' "De Rerum Natura," from which the title of the present book is borrowed: "Mortals live by mutual interchange. One breed increases by another's decrease. The generations of living things pass in swift succession, and *like runners in a race they hand on the torch of life.*"

It is, in fact, a universal rule of nature that the tissues of dead plants and animals undergo decomposition and are thus returned to the envelope of soil, water, and atmosphere at the surface of the globe. Should any component of organic life fail to decompose and be allowed to accumulate, it would soon cover the world and imprison in its inert mass chemical constituents essential to the continuation of life. Of this, however, there seems to be no danger. Experience shows that substances of animal or plant origin do not accumulate because they undergo, sooner or later, a chain of chemical alterations which break them down stepwise, into simpler and simpler compounds. It is in this fashion that after death the chemical elements are returned to nature for the support of new life. There is literal truth in the Biblical saying that "all are of the dust, and all turn to dust again."

The eternal movement from life, through organic matter, down to simple chemical molecules, and back into life again, is the biochemical expression of the myth of eternal return. Scientists have long been preoccupied with this complex cycle and have known that its continuation is essential to the maintenance of life on earth. The problem and its mystery are well stated in a note left by the illustrious chemist Antoine Lavoisier, shortly before he was beheaded by the French Revolutionists: "Plants extract from the air that surrounds them, from water and in general from the mineral kingdom, all the substances necessary to their organization.

"Animals feed either on plants or on other animals which themselves have fed on plants, so that the substances of which they are constituted originate, in final analysis, from air or from the mineral kingdom.

"Finally, fermentation, putrefaction and combustion endlessly return to the atmosphere and to the mineral kingdom the principles which plants and animals had borrowed from them. What is the mechanism through which Nature brings about this marvelous circulation of matter between the three kingdoms?"

Although the transformation of matter into life, and from life back to matter has long been recognized, its mechanism remained obscure until the beginning of the microbiological era. It was one of the greatest achievements of Louis Pasteur to show that organic matter undergoes decomposition through the agency of microbes, and that everything which once was living eventually returns to ash by way of microbial protoplasm. All the structures and products of life become food for countless types of microbes which make use of them in an orderly, progressive manner and which in turn die, thereby making the material from which their bodies were made once more available to other forms of life. Thus, microbes constitute indispensable links in the eternal chain that binds inanimate matter to life. They, too, play their part in passing on the torch of life.

During the past hundred years, scientists have gone far toward identifying the types of microbes involved in the natural cycles of the various chemical constituents of life. Even elementary textbooks illustrate, with elaborate, pictorial images, the various chemical steps through which carbon, phosphorus, and nitrogen pass from plant and animal to microbe and then back to soil, as in a cyclic dance. In a curious way, modern scientific findings are thus giving substance to some of the ancient myths of eternal return. Much more exciting, however, is the fact that scientific discoveries have revealed an aspect of life which had hardly been perceived in the past.

Living things do not behave as passive messengers when they transmit matter from one generation to the next or from one form of life to another. Passing the torch of life is truly a continuous act of creation. In fact, the torch of life is not passed as in a race. New torches are endlessly lighted from it, to be carried over all parts of the earth. And, mysteriously, during this process, in the course of aeons, living things have progressively become more varied and diversified through the operation of mutational and other evolutionary changes. There are, obviously, recurrent cycles and eternal returns, but there is also forward motion. The future does more than repeat the past. Awareness of this forward motion of life—called progress when applied to man—is perhaps the most distinctive feature of modern philosophy and science. It is what differentiates most profoundly the temper of modern times from that of all past ages, even the most enlightened.

Biological Progress

WHEREAS the belief in recurrent cycles—in a closed *circular* course of everything in the cosmos—fits the practical experience of men living in intimate contact with nature, the belief in progress as an expanding process endlessly generating new creations is of the nature of an intellectual *tour de force*. It demands a very long-range view of natural and human history, an awareness of the creative power of rational knowledge, and an almost blind faith in the wisdom of man. Belief in progress apparently began timidly in classical Greece, but it remained only a vague, unconvincing idea until the seventeenth century. Even Newton held to the traditional view of the stability and perfect design in nature and, therefore, could hardly conceive of biological and social progress. It was only after him that the sense of change and mutability began to grow. The belief in progress became a kind of religious faith among the philosophers of the Enlightenment with scientific inclinations; it has spread more and more vigorously ever since, weakening and almost destroying in the hearts and the minds of men the emotional power of belief in eternal return.

Granted that it is difficult to trace the precise origin of the idea of progress, there is no doubt that its final triumph coincided with the publication of Charles Darwin's revolutionary book *The Origin of Species*. Many reasons have been given to account for the unexpected and truly astounding popular success of this book. Its first edition of 1,250 copies was sold out on the day of publication (November 24, 1859). The second edition of 3,000 copies was also snatched, when it appeared six weeks later. The title certainly was not such as to have an obvious appeal for an unprepared lay public. Nor could the popular mind be excited by the detailed descriptions of minute differences between the varieties of animals found on small distant islands. In fact, the success of the book did not come so much from the approval of specialists as from an intense emotional response on the part of the cultivated public. To a large extent, the popular success was unrelated to the validity of the scientific evidence.

As pointed out by Stanley Hyman in *The Centennial Review, The Origin of Species* caught the imagination as if it had been a dramatic poem because it dealt with the ancient myth of the cycle of birth, struggle, defeat, triumph, resurrection, through examples taken from true nature. What impressed the vigorous and enterprising world of nineteenth-century England, was the account of competition between the various forms of life, ending in the survival of those best fitted to survive. This provided a symbol of man's own dominance over the rest of creation, and of the social dominance of the most gifted individuals within the human species. Most importantly, perhaps, Darwin's book made clear that the immense drama of competition not only represented the story of existing life, but, furthermore, accounted for the emergence —indeed for the creation—of new forms of life. Today, one century after the publication of *The Origin of Species*, its concluding paragraphs still evoke, as by a spell, Nature in the act of creation.

"It is interesting"—Darwin wrote—"to contemplate a tangled bank, clothed with many plants of many kinds, with birds singing on the bushes, with various insects flitting about, and with worms crawling through the damp earth, and to reflect that these elaborately constructed forms, so different from each other, and dependent on each other in so complex a manner, have all been produced by laws acting around us. These laws, taken in the largest sense, being Growth with Reproduction; Inheritance which is almost implied by Reproduction; Variability from the indirect and direct action of the conditions of life, and from use and disuse; a Ratio of Increase so high as to lead to a struggle for Life, and as a consequence to Natural Selection, entailing Divergence of Character and the Extinction of less-improved forms.

"Thus, from the war of Nature, from famine and death the most exalted object which we are capable of conceiving, namely, the production of the higher animals, directly follows. There is grandeur in this view of life, with its several powers, having been originally breathed by the Creator into a few forms or into one; and that, while this planet has gone cycling on according to the fixed law of gravity, from so simple a beginning endless forms most beautiful and most wonderful have been, and are being, evolved."

The idea that all forms of life are linked in some way was not original with Darwin. In fact, Arthur Lovejoy has shown in his book *The Great Chain of Being* that the Greeks, and all philosophers and scientists that fol-

lowed them, had recognized the existence of an unbroken
continuity among living forms—all the way from slimy
crawling creatures to animals and men. Before Darwin,
however, living forms were regarded as stable, immutable.
After him, this static concept was replaced by the dynamic theory that all existing forms had emerged from
earlier ones and are continuously giving rise to new
ones. The theory of evolution is supported by such an
immense body of facts, that it is now almost universally
accepted. On the other hand, there is still much uncer-
tainty as to the forces that bring about and direct the evolutionary changes.

Everyone accepts, of course, that mutations occur frequently, and that selection favors the multiplication of
the mutant forms best suited to live in a certain environment. The dual process of mutation and selection makes
it easy to imagine how differences between varieties have
come into being and have become stabilized. According
to Theodosius Dobzhansky, for example: "Three populations of the chaffinch, near Stuttgart, Germany, each
live in a definite neighborhood, and differ in the calls
which males utter in their breeding territories. One of
these populations is confined to a certain large park,
which is known to be about three hundred years old. It is
probable that the special 'dialect' of the chaffinches in
this part has evolved within this period of time."

Many similar adaptive changes of minor importance
have been observed, and some of them have also been
produced in the laboratory. But the more difficult problem is to account for the deep-seated changes which progressively generated all the species of creatures out of the
very primitive living forms, consisting only of undifferentiated molecules capable of reproduction. The orthodox view is that countless mutations occurred through
chance, and that the hundreds of millions of years during which life has existed have provided enough time for

the mutational changes to become sorted and organized by selective forces into all known living forms. There is, indeed, some mathematical evidence for this theory, but its real strength is that however implausible it may appear to its opponents, they do not have a more plausible one to offer in its place.

Another topic of intense controversy is whether evolutionary changes proceed toward a well-defined goal, or are the accidental result of blind forces. During recent years, the most eloquent spokesman for the former view has been the Jesuit anthropologist, Pierre Teilhard de Chardin. According to him, there exists a sort of diffuse universal consciousness throughout all creation. By a series of mutations this consciousness becomes better and better defined, more and more evident, as one goes up the scale of organization—from matter through all the living forms. In man the universal cosmic consciousness becomes self-consciousness, or thought. This evolution is still continuing and will eventually achieve a complete unity of mankind, a consciousness of the universe. Ultimately, evolution will reach the "Omega Point" determined by divine design. Thus, in Teilhard de Chardin's view, the direction of evolutionary changes is predetermined; there is only one direction, and ultimately it leads to God.

At the other extreme position are the biologists who believe that evolution has no goal and follows any direction that circumstances favor; in their view, evolution is entirely erratic and opportunistic. The transformations which led from the primordial living molecule to man were the result of one of the evolutionary directions, or rather of a variety of them in succession, for there was no sequence in a straight line. According to Darwin and his followers, evolution achieves its effects through struggle between competitive forms. According to the English writer Samuel Butler, and the Russian philosopher Kropotkin, evolution operates through cooperation and mutual help between organisms living at the same place and at the same time. In reality, as recently pointed out by Theodosius Dobzhansky, "Both competition and cooperation are observed in nature. Natural selection is neither egotistic nor altruistic. It is, rather, opportunistic."

Biological Partnerships

WHETHER evolution is goal-directed, or erratic and opportunistic, is a question of deep philosophical interest because it bears so directly on the meaning of life. On the other hand, the mere fact that evolution has occurred and continues to operate has a practical importance which is largely independent of its theoretical basis and of the mechanisms involved. One of the practical consequences of evolution is that living things are, in general, well-adapted to the physical and chemical conditions under which they have evolved and are likely to be misadapted when transferred to a different kind of environment. Another consequence is that they usually reach a remarkable degree of biological equilibrium with the other living things with which they have been associated during evolutionary development and, indeed, are often dependent on them for survival. It is this biological aspect of evolutionary adaptation that we shall now consider.

Herbert Spencer was one of the sociologists who found in Darwin's book a scientific justification for the competitive and aggressive character of the nineteenth-century capitalistic system. To him and to many nineteenth-century philosophers, the Darwinian theory meant that the really effective factor in organic evolution was the struggle for existence, resulting in the "survival of the fittest." The partisans of laissez-faire economics found a ready excuse for child labor, ruthless competition, and sweat shops in the words that they lifted out of context from one of Thomas Huxley's lectures: "From the point of view of the moralist the animal world is on about the same level as a gladiator's show. . . . The strongest, the swiftest, and the cunningest live to fight another day . . . no quarter is given." In truth, however, Huxley had also stated in his essay, "The Struggle for Existence in Human Society," that "The first men who substituted the state of mutual peace for that of mutual war . . . obviously put a limit upon the struggle for existence." It is apparent, also, that Darwin himself did not share the simple-minded view that devouring or being devoured was the essential mechanism of selection and of evolution. In *The Descent of Man,* he pointed out that "in numberless animal societies, the struggle between separate individuals for the means of existence disappears; struggle is replaced by cooperation."

More than any one else, it was the Russian philosopher and sociologist Kropotkin who first emphasized that cooperation and mutual help had been at least as influential as the struggle for existence in accounting for the facts of evolution. Kropotkin became the standard-bearer of this attitude through his book, *Mutual Aid, A Factor of Evolution,* published around the turn of the century. During his travels in Siberia and Manchuria, he had observed the frequent occurrence of cooperative endeavors in the animal world. Furthermore, the historical study of human institutions had convinced him that a desire for mutual aid had always prevailed among men. Many observers since Kropotkin have provided examples of cooperation among animals, hardly compatible with the popular view of the law of the jungle. There is overwhelming evidence indeed that pugnacity and aggressiveness are often less conducive to biological success than is the ability to "live and let live" and to cooperate with other individuals of the same or other species.

Mutual aid among animals is not, of course, based on sentiment. It corresponds rather to an instinct of preservation which gives to species and to individuals a better chance of survival under conditions of stress. This instinct is one of the complex and indirect results of evolutionary adaptation. Examples of biological cooperation among living things are found at all levels of development; they involve microbes and plants, as well as animals. Among animals an entertaining example is provided by the baboons in East Africa which have been recently observed in the wild by S. L. Washburn and Irven DeVore: "In open country their closest relations are with impalas, while in forest areas the bushbucks play a similar role. The ungulates have a keen sense of smell, and baboons have keen eyesight. Baboons are visually alert, constantly looking in all directions as they feed. If they see predators, they utter warning barks that alert not only the other baboons but also any other animals that may be in the vicinity. Similarly, a warning bark by a bushbuck or an impala will put a baboon troop to flight. A mixed herd of impalas and baboons is almost impossible to take by surprise." Thus, the social association between baboons and other species provides mutual protection.

Perhaps the most unexpected and picturesque display of cooperation among animals is that referred to as "cleaning symbiosis" which has been observed in a surprisingly large number of marine organisms. In recent years skin divers have discovered that certain species of marine animals specialize in cleaning others, a behavior that promotes the well-being of the cleaned animals and provides food for those that do the cleaning. Limbaugh has described as follows one particular case:

"One finds in the Bahamas the highly organized relationship between the Pederson shrimp (*Periclimenes pedersoni*) and its numerous clients. The transparent body of this tiny animal is striped with white and spotted with violet, and its conspicuous antennae are considerably longer than its body. It establishes its station in quiet water where fishes congregate or frequently pass, always in association with the sea anemone *Bartholomea annulata,* usually clinging to it or occupying the same hole.

"When a fish approaches, the shrimp will whip its long antennae and sway its body back and forth. If the fish is interested, it will swim directly to the shrimp and stop an inch or two away. The fish usually presents its head or gill cover for cleaning, but if it is bothered by something out of the ordinary such as an injury near its tail, it presents itself tail first. The shrimp swims or crawls forward, climbs aboard and walks rapidly over the fish, checking irregularities, tugging at parasites with its claws and cleaning injured areas. The fish remains almost motionless during this inspection and allows the shrimp to make minor incisions in order to get at subcutaneous parasites. As the shrimp approaches the gill covers, the fish opens each one in turn and allows the shrimp to enter and forage among the gills. The shrimp is even permitted to enter and leave the fish's mouth cavity. Local fishes quickly learn the location of these shrimp. They line up or crowd around for their turn and often wait to be cleaned when the shrimp has retired into the hole beside the anemone."

Experiments in which the cleaners had been removed from a certain area have demonstrated that "cleaning symbiosis" is of great importance in maintaining the health of the marine population. "Within a few days [after removal of the cleaner] the number of fish was drastically reduced; within two weeks almost all except the territorial fishes had disappeared. Many of the fish remaining developed fuzzy white blotches, swelling, ulcerated sores and frayed fins." When a "cleaner" shrimp was placed in the aquarium, it began immediately to clean the infected fishes.

The extent of cleaning behavior in the ocean illustrates

in a picturesque and striking manner that cooperation in nature is as important as the tooth-and-claw struggle for existence.

At a lower level among animals, the so-called Portuguese man-of-war illustrates a different kind of association. The remarkable thing about the Portuguese man-of-war is that it is not a single animal but a colony of separate organisms that have banded together in the course of their evolution. The part of the Portuguese man-of-war known as the float is one organism; another organism constitutes the fishing tentacles that capture plankton; a third kind carries out the digestive functions; etc. The various organisms do not live long when they are separated.

Insects enter into all sorts of intimate associations with plants and microbes. For example, the yucca flowers can be pollinated only by a certain kind of moth, and the larva of this moth can develop only in the yucca seed pods. The moth larva feeds on the yucca, and the moths pay for the food that they get from the yucca by insuring the cross-fertilization of its flowers. The fecundation of orchids by pseudocopulation with insects provides some of the most amazing illustrations of adaptive behavior, passed on from generation to generation through genetic mechanisms. The flower of the orchid, *Ophris speculum,* for example, resembles the body of the female burrowing wasp, *Scolia ciliata,* which lives on the same sand banks. The male wasp emerges from its burrow in March, one month before the female, and during its month of bachelorhood, it engages in pseudocopulation with the orchid and thereby brings about its pollination. Pseudocopulation also takes place between the wasp, *Lissopimpla semipunctata,* and the orchid, *Cryptostylis leptochila,* which attracts the male by smelling like the female insect.

The process of fusion of two separate organisms, as contrasted with fission of cells, in certain cases has a nutritional as well as a sexual aspect. Thus in *Trichonympha,* a symbiotic protozoan of roaches, the female cell or gamete to all intents and purposes "eats" the male gamete. Certain kinds of colonial ants cultivate particular species of mushrooms which have never been found growing anywhere except in the ant nests. The ants, in their turn, have become completely dependent on the fungus.

Termites live almost exclusively on wood, but they can digest it only because they harbor in their gut certain kinds of protozoa. If the protozoa are destroyed, as can be done by heat treatment, then the termites die of starvation. Similarly, bloodsucking insects always carry certain kinds of bacteria which help them to digest the blood constituents. In both these cases, the protozoa and the bacteria also are dependent on their hosts; they are unable to survive even if supplied with wood or blood, once they are removed from the termites or mosquitoes.

It is appropriate to recall here the fact mentioned earlier, that many kinds of insects—roaches and lice, for example—cannot develop in the absence of certain microbes which they harbor in specialized structures of their bodies from the time of birth.

There are also known many types of associations among various species of microorganisms. For example, the protozoan, *Paramecia bursaria,* is green because it normally harbors microscopic algae of the *Chlorella* species. The protozoan can be cured of "contamination" with these algae by treatment with certain drugs, but then it loses its green pigmentation and fails to develop full size. What might be regarded as an infection is, in fact, a successful and almost indispensable association!

While it is important to emphasize that cooperation is very common among living things in nature, it must be acknowledged that practically all living organisms eventually serve as food for others, and that many individuals must perish in order that the group survive. Granted this fact, there is, however, overwhelming evidence that the different forms of life exist in equilibrium under natural conditions. Although this equilibrium is never stable, it permits, nevertheless, the survival of most species under ordinary circumstances. While altruism may have no part in the interrelationships among living things, it is certain that selfish interest is best served by opportunistic tolerance.

Since most creatures live at the expense of some other, the chain that binds all forms of life is, in final analysis, forged out of dead bodies. Many curious facts have come to light illustrating the variety of the nutritional links which make up the chain of life. The records of the Hudson's Bay Company show, for example, great fluctuations at fairly regular intervals of years in the numbers of fur-bearing animals caught by trapping. These fluctuations reflect the availability of rodents on which the fur-bearing animals feed, and in turn the size of the rodent population is controlled by the abundance of crops, by weather, and by disease.

Likewise, the fish population fluctuates qualitatively and quantitatively in ocean waters under the influence of varied factors which affect the aquatic flora and fauna. The abundance of plankton and the kinds of plants and animals prevailing in it change continuously from season to season and from year to year. When the current from the Atlantic predominates, it brings to the English coast, water rich in phosphate, which favors one species of glassworm, and the result is a good herring year in Plymouth. In contrast, currents from the Channel bring in water poor in phosphate, resulting in the predominance of other animal species, and this causes failure of the herring fishery. All over the world, water movements affect the fish population indirectly but profoundly by controlling the abundance of small plant and animal life, which serves as food for the larger species.

Equilibrium in nature can be upset, not only by changes in the physical environment but also by disturbing the complex relationships that develop between different kinds of living organisms, after they have existed in close contact for prolonged periods of time. An odd illustration of this fact has recently been brought to light in patients treated with antimicrobial drugs. It is commonly observed that certain types of drug treatment bring about pathological disorders which indirectly result from elimination of the bacteria which are normally present in the tissues, especially in the intestinal and respiratory tracts. Disappearance of one kind of microbial population is rapidly followed by the development of another kind, and this change brings in its train unexpected and often dangerous consequences.

The difficulties that may follow antibacterial therapy are, in fact, similar in essence to those encountered in any attempt to control predators in nature. When rabbits became scarce in England following introduction of the myxoma virus which killed them, the foxes and birds of prey began to raid poultry yards. On the Kaibab Plateau, extermination of the wolves and mountain lions has proved unfavorable to the deer, because they became so numerous that they overgrazed their feeding areas, and thus suffered ultimately from undernutrition.

It is of interest to mention in this regard the observations on wolves and caribous recently reported by Lois Crisler in her book *Arctic Wild:* "The fit and healthy caribou, even the quite young fawns, are apparently able to outdistance the hunting wolves with comparative ease. In almost all cases investigated, it was found that the caribous killed were those hampered by disease, old age, or injury of some kind. The natural role of the wolf, in fact, is as the culler of the unfit. As a result wolf 'control' has had disastrous effects on the Nelchina herd of Alaskan caribou. From an estimated total of four thousand animals

in ten years the figure, without the limiting factor of wolf
predation, had risen to the startling total of about ten
thousand. The available winter range was no longer sufficient, and the consequent trampling and over-grazing
threatened the livelihood of the excessive caribou population."

Naturalists have become acutely aware, during recent
years, of the disastrous results that commonly follow disturbances in the biological equilibria between different
species, whether these disturbances be accidental or man-
caused. Any one interested in this problem can read in
The Forest and the Sea by Marston Bates and also in
The Ecology of Invasions by Animals and Plants by
Charles S. Elton, fascinating illustrations of the calamities
resulting from biological disturbances; these examples are
all very relevant to the modern world.

Modern studies on animal and plant populations have
clearly demonstrated the potential dangers attending the
excessive multiplication of any one species of living things.
They have revealed that Nature is not a chaos of warring
factions but a complex and delicate system of balances in
which all living things share and to which they all contribute. The consequence of this fact is that the richer a
natural community is in forms and species, the greater its
inherent ability to absorb shocks from the outside. In
other words, the greater the variety in a biological population, the greater its chance to survive and prosper.

Granted the fact that the existing population in a given
place at a given time does not necessarily represent a natural equilibrium, or the best possible state of affairs, it
remains true, nevertheless, that tampering with the bal-
ance of forces in nature is always risky, because unforeseeable consequences are likely to result. All living things
are bound together as in a net, or, more exactly, they
constitute a highly organized web of subtle but fragile
beauty. Human existence is enmeshed in this web, and it

is for this reason that conservation is much more than a sentimental issue, or a set of practical rules. Conservation expresses a creative philosophy of life derived from the fact that, throughout the world, all living things are inter-dependent.

THE QUALITIES OF MAN

The Humanness of Ancient Man

JUST AS we do not know what life is, yet can distinguish between an inanimate object and a living animal or plant, similarly we cannot give a scientific definition of man, yet we have no difficulty in differentiating him from even the most manlike monkey. One of the gross deficiencies of science is that it has not yet defined what sets man apart from other animals. It is true, of course, that much is known of the physical and chemical characteristics of the human body, and of its interplay with environmental forces; certain responses of the human mind to various stresses and experiences have also been extensively studied. Unfortunately, most of what has been discovered concerns only those aspects of human "nature" which man has in common with the rest of nature, as if he were just another animal. There is hardly any scientific knowledge of the traits which are peculiar to man and which enable us to recognize him instantly as we encounter him in the world today and as we find the traces that he has left in prehistoric sites. Man is recognized not so much by what he is, as by what he does, especially under the spell of his emotions and through the power of his intellect.

Ideally, the understanding of man should be derived from knowledge of his evolutionary past. But while the evolution of his body can be traced approximately one million years back, the early evolution of his cultures and, therefore, of his mind, is almost a closed book. The extent of our ignorance of these problems was highlighted by the international conferences on evolution that were held in 1959 to celebrate the publication of Charles Darwin's *Origin of Species*. The speakers at these conferences had a great deal to say concerning the evolution of plants and animals, but very little concerning the application of evolutionary theory to human beings and to human societies.

The oldest authentic evidence of human activity so far discovered are stone tools found in Africa which date from the Pleistocene, perhaps close to a million years ago. It appears certain, furthermore, that the making of tools was invented independently in the very distant past by different kinds of men. Expertly made tools became fairly common a hundred thousand years ago.

During the third interglacial period, Palestine seems to have been the geographic boundary between two different groups: *Homo sapiens neanderthalensis,* who lived in Northwest Europe, and another type more like modern man, *Homo sapiens sapiens,* who probably came from Africa. The inhabitants of Palestine may have been either hybrids or an intermediate population. It was approximately seventy-five thousand years ago, during the last Ice Age, that Neanderthal man, with his Mousterian culture, was replaced in Europe by the more modern type of man identified with the Aurignacian culture. The latter displaced the former probably because he had more efficient stone tools and probably used the bow and harpoon. In view of the fact that there have existed several kinds of ancient man, it is meaningless to ask where and when *Homo sapiens* first appeared. Mankind today contains genetic elements originating from several types of populations.

In many caves of Southern France and of Spain, there

have been discovered magnificent paintings and drawings which certainly date from Paleolithic times; they show all sorts of animals and a few men, with frequent hunting scenes. The caves have also yielded extraordinary statuettes of women, often designated as Paleolithic Venuses, most of which display exaggerated feminine characteristics. All these forms of art serve as evidence of the high level of the prehistoric Aurignacian culture which prevailed in Southern Europe some twenty thousand years ago. There is reason to believe that the caves which have yielded the Paleolithic paintings were the sites of certain ceremonies and rites with magical significance related to hunting and to fertility cults.

The existence of Paleolithic magic is a fact of human evolution probably more important for the understanding of man than is the physicochemical and biological knowledge of bodily structure—indeed, more important than is the development of tools. All animals have evolved both physically and physiologically. Certain animals, in addition to monkeys, have developed primitive tools—for example, a certain finch of the Galapagos Islands uses a cactus spine which it holds in its beak to poke into crevices of tree bark and thus dislodge worms on which it feeds. But only man—even very primitive man—has made drawings and sculptures of himself, of animals, and of plants, in the thought that he could thus influence events through magic.

The change from Paleolithic to Neolithic culture is a very obscure phase of human history. As far as is known, the earliest Neolithic men began to practice agriculture and to live in villages nine thousand years ago, first probably in the Fertile Crescent constituted by the valleys of the Euphrates and the Tigris. Recent archeological discoveries have made it possible to trace the spread of this Neolithic culture into Europe from its birthplace in the Near East. Among the most recent discoveries are those made near the village of Halicar on Turkey's Anatolian plateau, where a small mound has yielded remains of settlements extending over several centuries. The most remarkable finds in Halicar were clay statuettes, eight thousand years old, having some similarity to the Paleolithic "Venuses" found in the caves of Southern Germany, France, Spain, and Italy. Halicar statuettes represent the Anatolian "mother-goddess," which apparently was a fertility symbol.

Considered as a whole, the existent knowledge of prehistory makes it possible to construct a fairly continuous story of human migrations and human handicrafts over hundreds of thousands of years. But what first made *Homo sapiens* develop self-consciousness, plan for the future, and thus become qualitatively different from the rest of creation, is as mysterious as ever. The origins of man are hidden behind clouds of ignorance as thick as those that surround the origin of life. We know a great deal concerning the evolution of living things in general, but there is no factual information concerning the passage from matter to life, nor concerning the emergence of self-consciousness and of culture out of animal instincts. As pointed out by MacDonald Critchley, it is wise to remember that, "Even in the case of the most untutored, primitive savage human communities, the language system is so far removed in its complexity from the crude and simple utterances of the sagest of the primates, as to be scarcely comparable. And nowhere and at no time has there been any hint of an approximation between these two extremes. Can it be, therefore, that a veritable rubicon does exist between animals and man after all?"

As mysterious as the emergence of language is the fact, already mentioned, that the first known pictorial and sculptural representations of men and women suggest some form of magic. In the Paleolithic cave of the Trois Frères in Southern France, there was painted some fifteen

hundred years ago, a human being known among anthro-
pologists as the Sorcerer, because he obviously was intended to represent some magical function. His female
counterparts are the many paleolithic and neolithic statuettes of women thought to symbolize a fertility cult. In
the Anatolian neolithic site of Halicar, there were also
found in strategic places human skulls propped up with
stones in a manner which suggests that the inhabitants
practiced an ancestor cult. Furthermore, it is a remarkable
fact that from the most ancient times, man has buried his
dead with offerings as if he were concerned with some sort
of immortality.

All these spiritual activities point to the weakness of a
crudely materialistic concept of human evolution. They
make it probable that evolutionists, and scientists in general, will remain only on the fringe of the study of the
nature of man, if they continue to shut their eyes to the
nonmaterial aspects of his nature and insist on regarding
him as a mere animal. We shall emphasize repeatedly in
the following pages that man cannot be defined only in
terms of his animal characteristics and of his evolutionary
past. One could almost say that his genesis is understood
from his ends, rather than from his beginnings. In the
words of Aristotle, "The nature of man is not what he
is born as, but what he is born for."

Human Spirituality and
Self-consciousness

SCIENTISTS TEND TO emphasize the similarities between man and animals. As already pointed out,
they study the common denominators and points of identification rather than the differentiating features. This tendency became particularly strong at the end of the 18th
century, at a time when many philosophers contended

that the natural aspects of man could not be distinguished from those of subhuman creatures. Needless to say, the theory of evolution provided scientific support for this attitude.

The proponents of evolution through selection admittedly found it difficult to explain how morality and other spiritual traits which are genuinely human could have emerged from an entirely materialistic and opportunistic origin. Darwin recognized how doubtful it was that the offspring of the more ethical parents would be reared in greater numbers than the children of selfish parents, and for this reason he could not conceive that natural selection alone had been responsible for moral improvement. Nevertheless, he did believe that the moral sense had evolved. In a rather obscure way he contended that the moral sense had sprung from the interaction of unconscious social instincts with man's superior intellectual powers, and that the whole process had been guided by natural selection because morality had proved beneficial to the group in the long run. "It must not be forgotten," Darwin wrote in *Descent of Man,* "that although a high standard of morality gives a slight or no advantage to each individual man and his children over the other men of the same tribe, yet an advancement in the standard of morality will certainly give an immense advantage to one tribe over another."

During recent years many physiologists have come to believe that other traits which are characteristic of man, such as self-consciousness and free will, can also be brought within the fold of natural sciences and of the theory of evolution. The understanding of feedbacks and the knowledge of servomechanisms have provided some basis for a tentative scientific interpretation of the operations of the mind. Professor Homer Smith, for example, likens consciousness "to a television tube with a so-called long decay-time such that it continues to glow for a substantial period after it has been excited, and thus affords a continuous rather than a flickering image. Within the parameters of this image the conscious animal can relate past experiences to anticipate the future and react accordingly, and with respect to one or another of various possibilities which may be presented simultaneously. Insofar as selectivity enters into this reaction we may speak of 'choice' without giving this much abused word any metaphysical implications; and insofar as any of the alternative modes of action promote the organism's welfare, we may designate the resulting activity as 'self-serving.'

"From the perspective of evolution, then, we may venture a tentative definition of consciousness as awareness of environment and of self-revealed objectivity, by self-serving neuromuscular activity which exhibits choice between alternative actions and relates past experience to anticipated future. Whether the time-binding activity extends over a period of seconds or of years is immaterial to the cogency of the definition."

It must be emphasized, however, that many are those who question that physicochemical sciences, in their present form, can account for free will and consciousness. The skeptics are found not only among philosophers but also among scientists. And it is entertaining in this regard to contrast with the opinions of Professor Homer Smith, quoted above, those of another eminent American physiologist who believes that consciousness is an individual experience not yet explainable by physical theory. In Dr. Seymour Kety's view, not even the perception of color can be explained, even though we know so much about wave lengths and about the structure and properties of the eye and brain. "Where is the sensation of blueness?" asks Dr. Kety. "It is neither wave length, nor nerve impulse, nor spatial arrangement of impulses—it is richer and far more personal. A machine can be built to perform any function that a man can perform in terms of behavior, computation, or discrimination. Shall we ever know, however, what components to add or what complexity of circuitry to introduce in order to *make it feel?*" (italics mine).

In general, students of human evolution have not attempted to explain the precise mechanisms by which the traits peculiar to man have evolved from his animal origins. They seem to accept that evolution "transcended" itself under certain unspecified conditions. According to orthodox doctrine, consciousness developed through a chain of progressive and accidental changes in the course of time, thus giving man—in the words of Professor Dobzhansky —the ability "to replace the *blind* force of natural selection by *conscious* direction based on his knowledge of nature and on his values" (italics mine).

No one has expounded this view with greater conviction and eloquence than the celebrated English biologist, Sir Julian Huxley. It seems appropriate, therefore, to quote at some length from a recent address presenting a comprehensive picture in which the emergence of life and of mind were seen as special manifestations of a more general cosmic evolutionary process. The following quotation is taken from a lecture broadcast by Sir Julian in 1960 for the British Broadcasting Company: "We now believe with confidence, that the whole of reality is one gigantic process of evolution. This produces increased novelty and variety, and ever higher types of organization; in a few spots it has produced life; and, in a few of those spots of life, it has produced mind and consciousness.

"This universal process is divisible into three phases or sectors, each with its own method of working, its own rate of change, and its own kind of results. Over most of the universe it is in the lifeless or inorganic phase. On earth (and undoubtedly on some planets of other suns) it is in the organic or biological phase. This works by natural selection and has produced a huge variety of animals and plants, some astonishingly high organizations (like our own bodies, or an ant colony), and the emergence of mind.

"Finally man (and possibly a few other organisms elsewhere) has entered the human or, as we may call it, psychosocial phase, which is based on the accumulation of knowledge and the organization of experience. It works chiefly by a conscious selection of ideas and aims, and produces extremely rapid change. Evolution in this phase is mainly cultural, not genetic; it is no longer focussed solely on survival, but is increasingly directed towards fulfillment and towards quality of achievement."

A fair summary of orthodox evolutionary doctrine would seem to be that the biological phase of evolution involves the continuous invention of self-reproducing matter through the gene nucleic acid mechanism, whereas the human phase of evolution is characterized by self-reproducing mind. Genetic information merely provides the raw material for cultural evolution, which is based on a system of heredity different from that embodied in the genes. Cultural evolution depends on the cumulative transmission of experience, in other words, on tradition.

Man, the Hoping Animal

WHATEVER VIEW one may hold of man's achievements and future, there is no doubt that he is at present the most successful product of organic evolution. He is rapidly occupying all parts of the globe and transforming it to his own ends; he has achieved mastery over most other living forms; moreover, he is in the process of acquiring the kind of knowledge that will enable him to control the evolution of other living things, and even his own if he so chooses.

A few years ago Julian Huxley stated that man may

yet become the "business manager of cosmic evolution." This ambitious view of man's role becomes even more startling when one compares it with Darwin's statement quoted earlier, according to which the sense of moral responsibility is the product of blind natural selection. Barely one hundred years separate Darwin's from Huxley's statements, yet within this relatively short time, what was a materialistic view of the world has evolved into an idealistic concept. Man, truly, is an incorrigible moralist. In fact, he gives up his ancient religions only to create new ones. Julian Huxley himself stated in his lecture "The Faith of a Humanist," mentioned above, that religions are an essential aspect of human life because they "help man to cope with the problem of his place and role in the strange universe in which he lives. Religion, in fact, is the organ of man concerned with his destiny. It always involves the sense of sacredness or reverence, and it is always concerned with what is felt to be more absolute, with what transcends immediate, particular, everyday experience. It aims at helping people to transcend their petty or selfish or guilty selves."

It is clear that like most normal persons, whatever their religious and philosophical persuasions, scientists are convinced at heart that the human spirit is more complete and broader in scope than the whole of the physical evolutionary system. All worthy men, and not least among them the most materialistic scientists, prize love, truth, wisdom, and beauty above all the concrete realities of the world and are willing to sacrifice physical well-being for the sake of these abstract values. Moreover, one of the peculiarly human traits is to entertain the hope that the world can be made a better and a happier place. It is because man is a hoping animal that he is endlessly inventing new utopias in which he embodies his concepts of perfection. Thus, in final analysis, man is characterized not only by what he has inherited from his animal origin, but also

and indeed even more, by his hopes, by his ability to
imagine a future that fits his idealized concepts, and by his
willingness to make the necessary efforts to reach or create Paradise.

Logical Future vs. Willed Future

ONE MIGHT SAY that man became com-
pletely differentiated from his animal background when,
for the first time, he became conscious of his future and
deliberately planned accordingly. It is true, of course, that
all living things function as if they were concerned with
the future: the bird builds its nests before laying eggs,
and the squirrel stores nuts for the winter. Aristotle and
his followers saw in this fact evidence that the future is
in some way built in the very fabric of living things. In
contrast, most modern biologists believe that what appears to be a preordained future, is in reality, the product
of evolutionary processes working through the selection
of accidental hereditary changes. Wherever the truth may
lie, it is certain that in man as in any other living thing,
there pre-exists from the time of conception a set of
structures and of tendencies which condition the future.

Experience shows that no one can entirely escape the
forces of the environment in which he lives, and that man
is as much a product of nature as are other living things.
The great difference, however, is that he does not will-
ingly submit to nature, and that constantly, although with
more or less vigor and varying success, he tries to escape
from his bondage and to achieve freedom. For this reason,
the human future is in some respects fundamentally different from the ordinary biological future.

In practice, the word future is used to connote two very
different aspects of what is to come. On the one hand,
there is a future that happens because determined by

antecedent forces operating according to immutable and inexorable natural laws. One might call this the logical future which scientists have become more and more able to predict, especially since they have learned to use the probability and statistical theories in their forecasts. There is a built-in logic in all social as well as in other natural events, and it is this logical determinism which makes possible science and, to some extent, prediction.

In contrast to the logical evolution of human affairs, which is to a large extent predictable because built into their very fabric, there is another aspect which is almost unpredictable because it depends on the influence of persons. Most human beings naturally have opinions and a type of behavior derived from the community in which they live. They operate within the traditional framework and are like weavers who continue to work according to the same pattern from generation to generation. But now and then the pattern changes; emphasis shifts from one type of interest to another; tastes, manners, and goals become so profoundly transformed, that the doings of one period appear ridiculous or even meaningless to the following generations.

In histories of every civilization and of every country, one can usually recognize when a change in pattern occurred, and it is often possible to trace the change to one person or a few particular persons operating under a particular set of circumstances. For example, Mohammed's teachings and leadership shaped the future of Islam; the philosophers of the Enlightenment made personal freedom and material progress watchwords of Western civilization. In other words, the history of all human institutions is marked now and then by new departures which correspond to decisions whereby the community becomes committed to certain ventures and attitudes toward life. These *willed* departures are the great moments of human history.

Until our times, societies remained more or less static

for prolonged periods of time, and it was only in rare circumstances that there occurred departures from tradition. The experience of one generation was transmitted to the next, and the ideal was merely to improve the techniques and customs accepted by the community; this was achieved through tradition and through the educational system. Naturally, evolutionary changes always took place, but so slowly that they could be incorporated into tradition without much struggle or trauma. In fact, society was hardly conscious of these evolutionary changes, and it is for this reason that completely new departures were regarded as political or social revolutions, and that the resistance to them caused profound disturbances. Today, willed departures occur at an ever-increasing rate, and they affect a wider and wider range of human activities. Increasingly, also, mankind is aware that its choices and decisions affect not only the immediate but also the distant future. We know that while modern technology gives us the power to bring about the kind of future that we want, this is a privilege which entails a frightening responsibility.

Men have always had to make choices and to reach decisions. In the past, most of these retained a personal character and had only limited repercussions. In contrast, opinions, tastes, habits, and modes of behavior now rapidly spread through whole nations and continents, and usually they become converted into collective policies which involve everyone, and, as often as not, the future as well as the present. Thus, it has become imperative for the community to develop an awareness of the consequences of its choices and actions—lest it find itself engaged on a road from which there is no retreat.

Whether deliberately or not, we are in the process of *creating tomorrow*. We are not merely adding to the world of today; because of the power of our means of action, we are making a new world. To simply drift into new situations, to trust to chance even though chance be dignified by the name of evolution, is likely to lead us into a morass of drabness and confusion: at worst, it might be tantamount to collective suicide. But a choice involves goals, or at least some criteria as to the kind of world we should strive to create. Thus, in final analysis, any choice is determined by our concepts of human life and of man himself.

It is important, of course, for human happiness that engineers and scientists create material wealth; also, that physicians and sociologists help man function long and effectively in a prosperous world. But their work will be to no avail if we do not discover the formula of the good life. And the difficulty is that each generation must write its own formula. For all their sublimity, the teachings of Socrates and Plato appear now somewhat limited in their scope; the philosophy of the Enlightenment, too narrowly materialistic in its goals; and the Sermon on the Mount, too absolute and timeless for a world intoxicated with change. We are eager to change the world, we have the knowledge and the power to reach almost any goal; if we had the will, we could perform almost any task. But we arc not sure of our goals and will. As H. G. Wells wrote in *A Modern Utopia,* "Will is stronger than fact, it can mold and overcome fact, but this world has still to discover its will."

The Pursuit of Happiness

THE MAIN biological drives of animal life are quite apparent in the state of nature. The satisfactions of hunger, of sex, and of a few other natural appetites contribute to the survival of the individual and assure the proliferation of the species. Man clearly is still an animal in these respects. The experience in the concentration camps during the last World War revealed how close to

the surface are the animal aspects of human nature; the
crudest animal appetites often resumed control in the
behavior of the inmates who were exposed to shortages
of food and deprived of normal sexual satisfactions. Thus,
essential biological drives persist in man, and they come
to the fore whenever survival is threatened. Anything that
scientists learn concerning animal nature, therefore, helps
in understanding human nature.

At least as important as the drives that man shares
with animals are those that make human life different
from animal life, as it so obviously is. Under the circumstances of normal civilized life, the instincts and natural
appetites express themselves in a mild, disciplined form.
Moreover, they are modified by a multiplicity of desires
and urges which vary from civilization to civilization and
from time to time, and which often become overpowering
even though they may not be essential biologically. The
efforts that man makes in order to satisfy his essential and
nonessential needs are usually called the search for happiness, and this constitutes one of the main preoccupations
of mankind. Indeed, many believe that happiness is the
raison d'être of existence.

The signers of the Declaration of Independence regarded the pursuit of happiness as one of the birthrights
of man—the third member of the trinity of human rights
after life and liberty. Although they did not define what
they meant by happiness, one may presume from the
conditions then prevailing in the world that their requirements for a happy life were more modest than those of
modern America. They probably had in mind elementary
comfort, enough of the proper kind of food, relief from
drudgery, pleasant and stimulating companionship and
experiences, and a minimum of diseases. Above all, perhaps they longed for freedom to move, to act, to speak,
and to decide at every moment the course of their lives.
Such a blueprint of human existence had been drawn by

the philosophers of the Enlightenment, and it was the subject of the celebrated *Sketch for a Natural History of the Progresses of the Human Mind* which Condorcet published in 1794. For the past two centuries, political reformers and natural scientists have labored to convert into reality the concept of the Golden Age imagined so vividly by our eighteenth-century ancestors.

It is truly a prodigious fact that two centuries have been sufficient to create in the Western world, and especially in the United States, the age of plenty and of freedom that was but a vague political utopia at the time of the American and French Revolutions. If the signers of the Declaration of Independence and the eighteenth-century social philosophers had spelled out, in specific words, what they considered the essential requirements of happiness, it would probably turn out that their goals have now been reached, and that the objects of their aspirations have become part and parcel of everyday life in the United States. Yet it is plain enough that the era of plenty and of freedom has not yet brought happiness to the modern world! It is not even certain that happiness is more widespread or greater in the favored social classes than among the destitute. Material well-being and freedom obviously contribute to happiness, but they are certainly not sufficient in themselves. Out of fairness to the sagacity of the signers of the Declaration of Independence, it must be noticed that what they emphasized was not the right to happiness, but to the pursuit of happiness. They knew well that striving toward a worthwhile goal brings more satisfaction than reaching the land of Utopia. As Cervantes said, "The road is always better than the inn."

In reality, the word happiness is the source of much confusion because it refers not to a well-defined state but to a highly subjective attitude. To say that men want happiness is redundant, because it merely states that they want what they want—which leaves the question unanswered. That the good life is not necessarily the affluent life, with a maximum of sensual and intellectual satisfactions, appears from the fact that all cultures trim, constrain, and mold many of the natural human impulses. Men choose among all their possibilities; furthermore, they pare and whittle the chosen impulses to make them fit into a pattern that relates their own life to the life of their community.

Not uncommonly, asceticism and sacrifice give more meaning to existence than does the opulent life. The extreme manifestation of this attitude is found in certain oriental cultures for which the ideal way of life is meditative contemplation, a Nirvana independent of the outer world. For Western man, however, and probably for most men everywhere, happiness is identified with the vigorous pursuit of a purpose that each individual formulates for himself. The quality of happiness is an expression of the quality of the purpose.

Experience shows that no one can long derive contentment from exclusive concern with his own selfish pleasure. This is very apparent in the case of material luxuries because, as Shakespeare reminds us in *Henry IV*, surfeit of them always causes boredom and nausea.

> *They surfeited with honey and began*
> *To loathe the taste of sweetness, whereof a little*
> *More than a little is by much too much.*

Nor do intellectual activities provide lasting pleasure if exercised from a purely selfish point of view, just as a source of entertainment or personal gratification. To endure and retain their intensity, the pleasures of the intellect must usually be associated with a worthwhile purpose, be it service to mankind or understanding of the universe. Physical luxuries and intellectual luxuries are insufficient by themselves to create the happy life because,

for some mysterious reason, man needs to transcend himself. He needs a duty, a dedication to some cause other
than pleasure. He can find happiness only by pursuing
something beyond happiness, by striving to play as best
he can his role in the human drama, and thus fulfill his
true destiny. This is the profound truth behind the Biblical
saying: "Seek ye first the Kingdom of God and His
righteousness, and all these things shall be added unto
you."

Man into Mankind

To LOVE one's neighbor and help him in
hours of trial is a formula for the pursuit of happiness
which has been adopted by most great religions and ethical systems. Unquestionably, this formula provides one
of the most effective modes of fulfillment for man. Another way is to consider individual existence as part of a
great human undertaking that began long ago and will
continue long into the future. The fact that I am alive this
minute, and that I enjoy the experience of living, is mag-
nified by the conviction that even though I shall die, in
some way my experience will not be lost. I am a link in
a long chain of growth and learning which makes human
life the great creative adventure of the cosmos. This is
true despite the obvious fact that mankind has experienced many defeats, and that destructive forces have often
interrupted and even routed the forces of creation and
of growth. Granted so many false starts, failures, and
tragedies, nevertheless it is apparent that human life is
becoming larger, richer, endlessly continuing to evolve
toward a higher level of perception. For any one of us,
the experience of today may be trivial, but it is never
meaningless if we see it as a part of the great human
adventure that will bring the fulfillment of Paul's saying,

"The first man is of the earth, earthly: the second man is the Lord from heaven."

Moralists and sociologists bemoan the fact that many young people have no faith, nothing to live for; they trace the restlessness and disenchantment, so common in our times, to this lack of dedication. To believe that nothing counts except the experience of today, of the very moment, does indeed engender despair. The human condition has no meaning without the faith that mankind is progressively—even though erratically—raising its sights from earthly satisfactions to some more exalted goal. And this faith implies the duty for everyone to contribute his part to the uphill effort in which mankind is engaged.

Although these words are so vague as to appear almost meaningless, they express, in fact, a human faith which has been a creative force in many lands for thousands of years. Today almost all rational and educated human beings know that an effective world society is one of the most urgent needs, and that real interdependence between nations will be implemented when the majority of human beings accept subordination of group aim to the concerns of all humanity. Long before this economic and political concept of One World Society gained prominence, however, there existed an intuitive philosophical and religious persuasion that Mankind is not merely an abstract concept, but a living, throbbing reality.

Throughout ancient and modern thought there appears time and time again, almost as a haunting theme, the belief that individual human beings are part of a greater unity. Twenty-five hundred years ago, Aristotle ended his *Ethics* on the note borrowed from Plato that the fullest development of human nature leads men beyond human nature itself, to participate in what is deathless and eternal. The dream of the fusion of all men in Man, who is Christ, is, of course, the philosophical basis of Christianity. During a lecture in 1837, Ralph Waldo Emerson reformulated this concept by telling an ancient fable according to which the gods in the beginning divided man into men that he might be more helpful to himself, just as the hand was divided into fingers. This fable, Emerson said, symbolized the doctrine that there is One Man, and that one must take the whole society to find the whole man.

In a similar mood, H. G. Wells stated in *A Modern Utopia* that he had perceived "glimpses of a comprehensive scheme with all personalities becoming integrated as in a synthetic wider being, the great State, mankind, in which we all move and go, like blood corpuscles, like nerve cells, it may be at times like brain cells, in the body of a man." In fact, it is apparent that science is today creating conditions favorable for a unification of mankind and may, in the long run, integrate all communities into an organism of which all parts will be interdependent.

During recent years, the concept of the physical and spiritual unity of mankind has found a mystical expression in the scientific and philosophical writings of the anthropologist Pierre Teilhard de Chardin—the Jesuit father referred to earlier, who made distinguished contributions to the anthropological research in China which led to the discovery of Peking man. The most widely quoted of Teilhard de Chardin's books is *The Phenomenon of Man*. Although popular, this book is difficult to read because of its complicated and peculiar language, and also because the concepts that it tries to convey are often obscure. Nevertheless, *The Phenomenon of Man* has caught popular imagination and has been extensively reviewed by scientists—at times with admiration, at times with hostility, but never with indifference. Clearly its success is not due so much to the theories that it presents, as to the fact that it reaches deep into some intimate preoccupation of modern man.

Thinking as a scientist and as a Catholic priest, Teilhard de Chardin developed the belief that the whole universe is a sort of organism involved in a gigantic process of evolution—in a state of becoming, rather than simply being. He felt that the evolutionary processes of the cosmos cannot be described only in terms of their origin because they have a definite direction, their future trends being determined by their inherent possibilities and, of course, by their limitations. The trend, as he saw it, goes from *Pre Life,* meaning the material world, to *Life,* including all living things, to *Thought* which characterizes man. Thought is the highest expression of the evolutionary process. To a Martian observing our planet with instruments capable of detecting all kinds of waves, Teilhard de Chardin contended, the most striking impression would be "not the blue of the seas or the green of the forest, but the phosphorescence of thought."

Considered as a step in the evolutionary process, man is not an isolated unit lost in the cosmic solitudes; neither is he the center of the universe; rather he is the "arrow pointing the way to the final unification of the world in terms of life." Man, furthermore, cannot be conceived of as alone. When first recognized in prehistory, he already "is a crowd" and it is one of his fundamental characteristics to function not as an individual but as a complex social body. The earth's roundness has been of importance in this regard by causing an intensification of psychosocial activity. The physical limitations of the earth have compelled increasing contacts between human thoughts, which instead of being thinly spread and scattered are becoming increasingly organized into a web with meaningful patterns. As the world population increases, and as means of communication are improved, idea encounters idea, and the human mind tends to become one great unity, which is Mankind. The ultimate end of evolution in Teilhard de Chardin's view is the final state which he calls the Omega point, where all will be unified in a "hyperpersonal" organization.

As pointed out by Julian Huxley in his laudatory preface to the English translation of *The Phenomenon of Man,* this view of human evolution is not as distressingly impersonal as appears at first sight. Teilhard de Chardin emphasized that the more evolved human being is one who, on the one hand, becomes more highly individualized, and who achieves, on the other hand, a high degree of conscious integration with other men. The evolution of man thus reveals two simultaneous and complementary trends: one toward keener awareness of self, and the other toward more intensive cooperation and participation.

One may feel impatient with the mystic and obscure scientific paraphernalia which shrouds Teilhard de Chardin's writings. One cannot help admiring, however, the manner in which he suffused with a warm glowing light the factual knowledge of the nature of man, and the aspirations for his future.

Chemically, as we have seen in a preceding chapter, man is very much like other living things, even like the most lowly microbe. Anatomically, he bears a striking resemblance to the higher animals, and especially to some apes, even with regard to the structure of his brain. As in all animals, the human brain consists of two main parts differing profoundly in functions. The hypothalamus is essentially like that which exists in all vertebrate animals; it is concerned with emotions, the selfish and predictable part of behavior. The cerebral cortex increases in size and importance as one goes up the animal scale, and it reaches its maximum in man; it is concerned with judgment, reasoning, foresight, consciousness. Thus, man differs from animals by the greater development of his brain. In addition, he uses tools that extend the range and sharpness of his senses and the power of his organs for action. He has even developed electronic computers that perform much faster than he can some of the functions of his brain. Most important, perhaps, he has created social institutions which supply the stability needed for long-term operations. They enable him to carry out programs involving enormous numbers of persons and lasting for periods of time much longer than his own life. Farming called forth the various institutions of real property and of land tenure; manufacture and commerce gave rise to banks; education became a continuous process through organized schools. Thus, human evolution is primarily a self-conscious psychosocial process based on the cumulative transmission of experience, of systematic knowledge, and of practical creations. The whole interthinking humanity might become a real organism, if it could develop institutions capable of acting as its sense and effector organs, and a coordinating central structure analogous to a dominant brain. The United Nations is an effort in this direction, and its ineffectiveness in the field of power politics should not blind one to the fact that several international organizations of a more technical character do function well and usefully—for example, World Health Organization and UNICEF. After all, the brain is the last organ to have developed in the course of biological evolution, and the General Assembly of the U.N. is only twenty years old.

It should be remembered, furthermore, that human institutions evolve just as do other living organisms. Ordinary living things evolve through the production of mutants which are like trial runs to be sorted out by natural selection. In a somewhat analogous manner, the various utopias—political, social, economic—are the working hypotheses of mankind to be tested for survival under the real conditions of life. Most of the utopias fail and disappear entirely because they are not adapted to the time and the place. Some, however, survive and they undergo progressive modification until they have achieved some approximate fitness to the environment. Interbreeding between different social structures also takes place, as is observed at present, between capitalist and collectivist societies. We shall discuss in the following chapter some of the human factors involved in the evolutionary growth and decay of human institutions. Suffice it to emphasize here that *duration* is one of the great life values. In Teilhard de Chardin's picturesque language, duration can be regarded as "biological space time" because it makes it possible to organize in a continuous and integrated structure all the human efforts which, linked together during eternity, eventually will make Mankind.

THE ADAPTABILITY OF MAN

The Open Future

THE LARGE CITIES of the modern world remind one of beehives and of ant hills. Each individual person in them has a specialized function and returns to rest at a particular place—as if he were but one among so many other interchangeable units in an immense colony. As human societies become larger, older, and more dependent on technology, the colonial organization becomes more intricate and less flexible. The formal resemblance between human institutions and the colonies of social insects is indeed so striking that one might conclude that modern man is doomed to become a specialized worker or soldier in a stereotyped social machine. Fortunately, the formal resemblances are misleading, because human societies differ in a fundamental way both in origin and in structure from all known insect colonies. Whereas each of the latter represents a gigantic single family, human societies in contrast represent groupings of many families. Whatever their degree of specialization, all the members of a given insect colony are but as many brothers and sisters from the same parents. The members of human groups are bound by social ties, but they differ in genetic make-up.

The great genetic diversity of human beings in most

94

parts of the world provides an immense range of potentialities for evolutionary development. Furthermore, as we have seen, evolution in man is now primarily of a psychosocial nature, and the great density of human populations increases enormously the rate of change by facilitating contacts and cross-fertilization of ideas. We have seen also that two types of changes, which appear at first sight contradictory, seem to be occurring at the same time. On the one hand, individual human beings become more and more differentiated; on the other hand, all of them become increasingly integrated into complex social structures. For this reason, human societies are not likely to achieve the state of almost complete stability which is made possible by the rule of instincts in insect colonies. But while it is certain that human societies will continue to evolve, the unsolved problem is to determine the direction in which they evolve or should evolve.

In many ways, the formulation of adequate goals for social development is now far more difficult than it was during earlier phases of civilization. In the past the production of food, shelter, and clothing, the limitation of physical effort, the control of all forms of suffering, constituted well-defined objectives which could be reached by technological improvements. The pursuit of knowledge for its own sake was also simpler. Scholars worked individually on questions that interested them. Receiving little recognition or help from the community, they had much intellectual freedom in the selection of their field of endeavor. The situation is now different because the elementary problems of survival have been solved, and also because the scientist has become a paid servant of the state. As a result, the question of what to do next, which used to concern chiefly the individual person, now must be considered by the social group as a whole.

We have enormous resources and powerful means of action. The difficulty is to choose what is most worth

doing among all the things that can be done and should
be done. Should we increase further the comfort and ease
of life; abolish more completely all forms of suffering and
of effort; strive for deeper knowledge and understanding
of the universe or for greater esthetic appreciation; achieve
more intimate communion with the cosmos; try to bring
about a true brotherhood among men? All these purposes, and many others, are worthy of human effort, but
they cannot all be pursued simultaneously with equal
vigor. There have to be choices, and these will have to be
based on judgments of value.

The nearer man comes to complete mastery of the
physical world, the more urgent it is for him to imagine
further worthwhile goals. The alternative is spiritual
stagnation, failure to find outlets for human energies and
talents, and in the end, boredom and unhappiness. It is
of some interest in this regard that sociological studies
are beginning to detect evidence of minor but significant
changes in the goals of the American society. Recent sur-
veys have shown, for example, that many American males
are becoming less concerned with the economic well-
being of their dependents and more likely to emphasize,
instead, problems of interpersonal relationship: such as
fulfilling the manly role at home, guiding the family,
spending more time with the children, etc. This shift from
economic to other human problems in the male population is recent and might have far-reaching implications if
the trend continues. The sociologist, W. W. Rostov, went
as far as suggesting, in his book *The Stages of Economic
Growth* that the trend toward larger families in the
United States derives in part from a desire to recapture
some aspects of the "strenuous life," now that the desire
for material conveniences has been almost satiated!

The possibility in the Western world to satisfy most of
the physical needs essential for pleasant living signifies
that mankind is about to reach one of its evolutionary

peaks. Clearly, however, evolutionary trends other than the search for comfort began long ago. Artistic expression dates at least from the Paleolithic era—twenty thousand years ago!—and yet it does not correspond to any material necessity. The pursuit of pure knowledge is also very ancient; theoretical science was studied even when it had no apparent practical applications, and there would still be many theoretical scientists today even if they were no longer needed for the technological development.

It is certain, therefore, that one can conceive of many possible evolutionary directions for human societies. In final analysis, these directions will be determined by judgments of value as to what makes life worth living. But equally important is the fact that the growth of all forms of knowledge will certainly suggest new goals and values of which we are not yet aware. Cultivation of the arts educates instinctive perceptions and thus helps revealing harmonious relationships in nature. Philosophy and the sciences of man render more sophisticated the sense of human brotherhood and of the meaning of life. Physical sciences add new sense organs to mankind, thus broadening and intensifying the awareness of the cosmos.

In principle, there is nothing new in the enlargement of human awareness that we are witnessing at present. It is a process which has been going on for thousands of years. In practice, however, there is the difference that, because of improved communications, almost every new experience and perception now becomes available to almost all of mankind. Needless to say, experiences and perceptions are distorted as they spread through the general public. But the important thing is that they are not lost, and that even in their distorted version they do affect tastes, opinions, and, in the end, goals. The result is that now, much more than in the past, men are exposed to an immense range of possibilities. The consequences of this

new situation are not predictable, except for the certainty
that the future of human societies is entirely open because new evolutionary trends are bound to develop from
the emergent novelty.

The fact that the future is open and unpredictable has
large medical and educational implications. As we shall
now see, it makes of adaptability the key concept in all
the problems posed by the care of the body and the
cultivation of the mind.

Health as Adaptability

ACCORDING TO encyclopedias, health is a
condition free of disease and of discomfort in which the
body and the mind are normal and function well. In practice, however, the word health cannot be defined in such
abstract terms because it refers to very different states,
depending upon the environmental conditions as well as
the professional requirements and the aspirations of each
particular person. For example, to be healthy means
something very different for a Chinese farmer, an American business man, the pilot of a supersonic plane, a Bene-
dictine nun, or a fashion model in Paris.

The traditional role of medicine and of public health
has been to prevent or correct, as far as it is possible, the
accidents and malfunctions of the body and of the mind
which interfere with human activities, and which shorten
life or render it less pleasant. Experience has shown, however, that as one social disease is rooted out, another one
springs up to take its place, and there are good reasons
to believe that this state of affairs will continue to plague
mankind as long as the conditions of life will continue to
change. In this respect, physicians and public health of-
ficers are like gardeners and farmers who have to fight
weeds and pests. Their work is never finished, and they

must continuously adapt their techniques to new problems.

Who could have dreamed a generation ago that over-
nutrition and hypervitaminoses would become common
forms of nutritional disease in the Western World; that
the cigarette, automobile exhausts, other air pollutants,
and ionizing radiations would be held responsible for the
increase in certain types of cancer; that the introduction
of detergents and various synthetics would increase the
incidence of allergies; that advances in the use of drugs
and other therapeutic procedures would create a new
pattern of infections; that alcoholics and patients with
various forms of medically induced disease would oc-
cupy such a large number of beds in the modern hos-
pital; that an eminent British epidemiologist could refer
to some maladies of our times as "pathology of inactiv-
ity" and as "occupational hazards of sedentary and light
work"? Since we can take it for granted that everything
will continue to change, endlessly, ideal health will always remain an ever receding mirage. Perfect harmony
between man and his environment could have existed only
if there had been a time when the world was stable and
ideally suited to human needs. But the Golden Age is
only a legend, and there is no hope that it will ever come
to pass in a utopian future.

Christopher Columbus expressed admiration, in the account of his travels, for the beautiful physical state of the
natives he had found in the West Indies. Captain Cook,
Bougainville, and the other navigators who discovered the
Pacific islands also marvelled at the state of health of
Polynesians at that time; and similar reports came from
travellers who first saw the American Indians in the
Great Plains and in the Rio Grande Valley. Ever since,
the experience of explorers has been that most primitive
people living in isolated communities are vigorous and
happy as long as they retain their ancestral ways of life,

whereas physical decadence sets in within one generation after they come into contact with white men. On the basis of these facts it seems fair to state that the health of primitive people, like that of animals in the wild state, depends upon some sort of equilibrium with their environment, and that it breaks down when the conditions of their existence suddenly change. What is true of primitive people also applies to civilized man. The general statement can be made that health depends upon fitness to the environment; it involves a state of adaptiveness.

New diseases appeared among the Polynesians, the American Indians, and the Eskimoes after they came into contact with Western civilization, because changed circumstances created new adaptive demands for which these people were not prepared. Thus the state of adaptiveness is only one of the components of health; another is the physiological power to react rapidly and effectively to the difficult and unforeseeable situations which occur inevitably whenever the social equilibrium is disturbed. The need for adaptability is especially critical in dynamic societies where living conditions are in a constant state of flux.

The more complete the human freedom, the more open the future, the greater the likelihood that new stresses will appear—organic and psychic—because man himself continuously changes his environment through technology, and because endlessly he moves into new conditions during his restless search for adventure. The state of adaptiveness to ancient agrarian societies proved almost useless under the conditions created by the nineteenth-century Industrial Revolution. The Western world has now reached an acceptable state of adaptiveness—social, emotional, and physical—to the type of industrial and urban life that emerged from the 19th century, but this is only a transitory state. New problems are being created at present by the countless and profound changes resulting from the second Industrial Revolution, and men will have to develop a new adaptive state in order to function effectively in the Automation Age.

Changeability is more and more the dominant factor in human life. In fact, one of the few unchangeable aspects of the human condition is that man must struggle to adapt himself to the ever changing environment. There is nothing tragic in this situation nor is it peculiar to man. It is the fate of all living things, and it is indeed the law and the very essence of life. However, granted the universality of change, it must be recognized that the problems of adaptation are presently taking a somewhat different aspect for the human race.

In the past, the changes in the conditions of life were generally slow, and it took several generations before they could affect all parts of the world and all social classes. This slow tempo made it possible for the full spectrum of adaptive forces to come into play. The physiological and even the physical characters of the body became progressively altered in order to meet the new conditions as did the social customs and the mental reactions. In contrast, technology now upsets the conditions of life so fast and its effects become so widespread all over the world that the biological and social processes of adaptation cannot occur rapidly enough to keep pace. It is becoming more and more difficult for the social body to achieve equilibrium with the new forces that it sets into motion and to which it is not adapted. Biologically and socially, the experience of the father has become almost useless to the son.

For man, adaptation involves his expectations—both his dreams and his fears. Furthermore, each person is a member of the human brotherhood, and the concept of health therefore implies a large component of social responsibility. To be completely successful, adaptation should in consequence contribute to the performance and

CARL A. RUDISILL LIBRARY
LENOIR RHYNE COLLEGE

the growth of the social group as a whole. It is essential to remember in this regard that the medical consequences of many of our present social activities will become manifest only in the years to come. Who can foretell the distant consequences of the fact that modern man no longer experiences the inclemencies of the weather, need not engage in physical exertion, can use drugs to allieviate almost any form of pain, and increasingly depends on tranquilizers and stimulants to live through the day? These achievements have, of course, made life easier and often more pleasant, but they may bring about an atrophy of the adaptive mechanisms which continue to be essential for the maintenance of health.

The usual definitions of health are therefore incomplete, because they consider the problem from an egotistic and static point of view. These definitions are formulated only in terms of the individual person, whereas they should consider also the collectivity. They are concerned with the present instead of emphasizing the future. They regard health as a state, although what matters most is the dynamic adaptability to the environmental factors which affect behavior and well-being. As already mentioned, these factors will continue to change quantitatively and qualitatively as long as the human condition continues to evolve. For this reason, the most important and interesting aspect of health is not its state but its potentiality. Just as wars have been won not with the weapons available at the beginning of the conflict, but with the new ones built out of potential resources as they were needed, similarly, health is the expression of the extent to which the individual and the social body maintain in readiness the resources required to meet the exigencies of the future.

The concept of health outlined in the preceding paragraphs implies, naturally, the freedom to choose, and the possibility for man to will his future within the limits imposed by natural forces. To believe in free will is, of course, a matter of faith, but what is certain is that man has a large reserve of adaptive potentialities from which to draw, if he has freedom to choose. Among mammalians, man is distinguished by a lack of biological specialization. This has enabled him to live under a wide range of climatic conditions; to eat many kinds of foods; and to engage in countless occupations. His future will measure up to his past only if he can retain the ability, the desire, and the will to carry on his adaptive evolution and thus meet successfully the new trials that he will certainly have to face. Greater knowledge of the range of adaptive potentialities in the human species, and the development of techniques for strengthening them, thus constitute the scientific basis for the health of the future.

Genetic Control of the Human Stock

UNDER NATURAL circumstances, plant and animal populations become adapted to their environment through the selective reproduction of the biologically successful mutant forms. In man also, natural selection has operated in the past and continues to operate at the present time. There is no doubt that profound changes can occur in the genetic endowment of man—as illustrated by the differences in physical and physiological characteristics between populations living in the arctic, and those adapted to the tropics. To a large extent, the ability to master intellectual and behavioral problems is also an innate endowment. It is built in the genetic apparatus just as is resistance to physical and mental stresses. The human child begins to smile at three months of age, independently of any training or fondling; the eagerness to play and to explore also seems to be genetically inherited, as well as are other patterns of intelligence of response to the environment.

Hereditary changes in man have resulted so far from undirected processes, blind selective forces tending to favor the survival of the persons best fitted to a given environment. A few geneticists believe, however, that the time has now come to control scientifically the evolutionary changes, in order to prevent the degenerative effects of civilization on the human stock. Whereas mutation rates are increasing, our ways of life are interfering with the elimination of undesirable genes; natural selection is more and more embarrassed by social and medical practices. True enough, the genetic processes of degeneration are so slow, that one is tempted to shrug off their effects, because most of them take hundreds of years to become evident. As in the case of erosion they come to be accepted as a part of the natural order. Social scientists and men of affairs are no more interested in such remote problems than is the general public. The fact is, however, that the most destructive, as well as the most creative operations of the living world, have been of a creeping, secular character. In the long run they are probably the most influential determinants of the future of the human race.

In view of these facts, it would seem logical to take advantage of modern biological knowledge and attempt some measure of control over the hereditary endowment of man. The celebrated American geneticist H. G. Muller has recently made concrete proposals to this effect. What Professor Muller suggests is simply the widespread practice of artificial insemination, using for this purpose preserved sperm obtained from human males whose life record is well known. In his view, this policy of positive eugenics would facilitate the spread through the general population of a number of desirable genetic characters, including physical and intellectual endowments.

Professor Muller's program of positive eugenics has stirred up passionate controversies, and there is as yet no indication that it will be applied on any significant scale. Objections to it come from two very different angles. First is the fact that genetic science is not yet sufficiently developed to permit prediction of what will happen if steps are taken to control human evolution. Many geneticists take, in this regard, a position almost completely opposite to that of Professor Muller; they claim that far from trying to channel genetic make-up in certain directions, we should maintain as much genetic diversity as possible. It is important, according to Professor P. B. Medawar, to "maintain a population versatile enough to cope with hazards that change from time to time and from place to place. A case can be made for saying that a genetical system that attaches great weight to genetic diversity is part of our heritage, and part of the heritage of most other free living and outbreeding organisms." Instead of trying to tailor man to a future which is at best dimly visualized, it is probably wiser at this stage to develop a culture fitted to man's needs.

The other fundamental objection to positive eugenics is that no one really knows what characters to breed in order to improve the human stock. Everyone agrees, of course, that it would be desirable to eliminate certain obviously objectionable traits, such as gross physical and mental defects—though even this limited program poses problems of judgment and of execution far more complex than is usually realized. But the selection of positive qualities raises questions of a much more subtle nature.

It is relatively easy to formulate a genetic program aimed at producing larger pigs, faster horses, better hunting dogs, or more friendly cats. But what is the ideal for human societies? The cave man, for all his strength and resourcefulness, would not get along well in a modern city. On the other hand, our present way of life may soon be antiquated, and future life may demand a kind of endurance undreamt of at the present time. For all we know, resistance to radiation, to noise, to intense light, to the monotony of continuous stimuli, and to the eternal repetition of boring activities, may become essential for biological success in future civilizations. Who knows, furthermore, whether mankind is better served by the gentleness of Saint Francis of Assisi and Fra Angelico or by the dynamism of the Industrial Revolution and modern art? Is the higher type of society one which prizes, above all, individual and self-development, or one which regards devotion to the common welfare as the highest standard of morality? Is it at all desirable to reproduce on a large scale a trait the appeal of which is perhaps its uniqueness? How many Beethovens would it take to make his genius commonplace? Furthermore, would a human being endowed with Beethoven's genes have the kind of musical genius that would enable him to express the moods of the automation age?

The fundamental difficulty in formulating a program for the genetic improvement of man is that we do not know what we are nor where we are, what we want to become nor where we want to go. In fact, mankind has not yet developed the skill to think effectively about these problems. To a large extent we still hold to a static and mechanical view of the universe and of life. The discussions about evolutionary development rarely encompass a continuously emergent novelty, an open future, not predictable from what is known. Yet this is probably the most profound meaning of the evolutionary concept —a view of life as a continuous act of creation, in which man has become the most important actor.

The Cultivation of Existing Potentialities

WITHOUT RESORTING to genetic manipulation, man can train himself to be more effective and more creative. Every person has in reserve a wide range of potentialities—both physical and mental—which remain unexpressed. As is well-known, any one can, with a little systematic effort, become better at almost any task, and more resistant to almost any kind of stress. Because the dominant trend in our civilization has been to control the environment, little has been learned of the extent to which it is possible to modify, by systematic and continued effort, the human machine and the human mind. Nevertheless, there are a number of isolated facts which point to large possibilities in this direction.

Experiments with laboratory animals have shown that it is possible by adequate stimulation to tune up the organism for more rapid and more efficient responses to the environment, such as: release of certain hormones, development of adaptive mechanisms, production of antibodies. Exposure to various forms of stimuli and stresses, during the very early stages of development, renders the animals sturdier, emotionally more stable, and more efficient at learning tasks. Particularly striking is the fact that the ability to learn is conditioned by early exposure to the proper kind of stimuli. This has been shown by measuring the ability of rats to perform in a maze and observing the eagerness with which they explore an unknown environment. The intelligence and intellectual curiosity of rats handled frequently during the first twenty days of life is greater than that of animals which have not been stimulated.

Baby chimpanzees kept in the dark for a few months after birth, later on have greater difficulty than ordinary animals in recognizing colors and shapes, even though their eyesight is completely normal. A similar situation is observed in human beings who lacked pattern vision in childhood. Even though the eye defect can be corrected by removing an opaque lens or transplanting a clear cornea, these persons experience great difficulty in learning to distinguish a square from a circle, visually. The fact that adequate stimulation of the organs and of the mind is essential for human development is forcefully illustrated by the examples of so-called "wolf children" found in the wilderness after being abandoned without human contact for several years. These children have had great difficulty in learning the most elementary gestures and reactions of civilized behavior.

As already mentioned, little is known of the extent of human potentialities, because the trend of civilization has been to control and modify the external environment for the sake of comfort, the ideal goal being total elimination of effort and suffering. We do little, if anything, to train the body and soul to resist strains and stresses; but we devote an enormous amount of skill and foresight to conditioning our dwellings against heat and cold, avoiding contact with germs, making food available at all hours of the day, multiplying laborsaving devices, dulling even the slightest pain with drugs, and minimizing the effort of learning. The enormous success of these practices in making life more pleasant and more effective, has, unfortunately, led to the neglect of another approach for dealing with the external world, namely, the cultivation of the resources in human nature which make man potentially adaptable to a wide range of living conditions.

There is at present little scientific knowledge concerning the mechanisms involved in adaptation, and this ignorance makes it difficult to formulate the problem rationally. Nevertheless, there is reason to believe that science can develop techniques conducive to greater adaptability and yet compatible with the values of civilized life. This belief is based on the fact that Nature itself is the great healer. There exist in the body many natural systems of defense which protect the various organs and functions against most forms of injury—whether these originate from nature or from technological civilization. If man can really learn to cultivate and enhance his defense mechanisms, he will be better able to function pleasantly and effectively in the new world he is creating. Furthermore, development of these potentialities may soon become essential, because it is futile to hope that the environment can be controlled sufficiently to assure passive health and happiness. More and more, adaptation will be an active process demanding continuous efforts.

Many of the stresses that man encounters in the modern world affect the mind first and the body only secondarily. For this reason, adaptive mechanisms having their seat in the mind are as important as those affecting the body machine. Man can learn by experience to resist suffering, to make intellectual efforts, to overcome impatience, to manifest activity. A society which depends on sedatives or stimulants to continue functioning cannot achieve the state of resilience necessary for survival, let alone for growth.

The need to regard adaptation as a creative process involving continuous effort applies also to the process of learning. In a world where everything changes rapidly, the practical facts learned in school soon become obsolete. The techniques and equipment which are the most up-to-date expression of knowledge during the school years are usually outmoded by the time the student begins to function in adult life. The only knowledge of permanent value is theoretical knowledge, and the broader it is, the greater the chances that it will prove useful in practice because applicable to a wide range of conditions. The persons most likely to become creative and to act as leaders, are not those who enter life with the largest amount of detailed, specialized information, but rather those who have enough theoretical knowledge, critical judgment, and discipline of learning to adapt rapidly to the new situations and problems which constantly arise in the modern world.

These qualifications are not acquired without effort, and may even demand painful effort. In fact, it may well be dangerous to make learning passive and effortless, because one of the most important aspects of education should be to instill the willingness to engage in difficult intellectual work. Like health, learning cannot be acquired passively. It is an active process, and the measure of its success is the extent to which it enables the individual to adapt to the unpredictable circumstances of life and thereby to meet them successfully.

To a large extent, willingness to make an effort depends, of course, on the perception of some sort of a goal. The increased prevalence of juvenile delinquency highlights that adaptation for man in the modern world cannot be defined only in terms of physical fitness but must take into consideration goals and position in society. It is a painfully ironical fact that legislation and social mores tend to prolong the period during which young people are treated as if they were immature and irresponsible, precisely at the time when children are growing faster and physically maturing earlier. Vigorous and well-fed young people need activity, while society urges on them a sheltered and effortless life. They are eager to show their worth and to function usefully, while labor laws bar them from employment. They crave an imaginative life and the chance to manifest initiative, while all forms of responsibility are denied them because they are regarded as children.

It would be entertaining, if it were not tragic, to contrast the place occupied in our society by the modern fully-developed, six-foot teenagers with that occupied by their equivalents in the past. Throughout history, young adults have acted effectively as active members of po-

litical parties, creators of business enterprises, advocates
of new philosophical doctrines, or even as leaders in warfare—whereas modern young people are expected to find
fulfillment in playgrounds, juke boxes, and passive diver-
sions.

Because young people are potentially as able, enterprising, and worthy as those of the past, it is pathetic
that society does not offer them the challenge they de-
serve and the chance to formulate goals of their own
choosing. This social attitude contributes to rendering
them more likely to yield to sexual impulses, become
juvenile delinquents, or turn to philosophies of despair.
Society must recognize that fully-developed, well-fed
young bodies with active minds, need some satisfying and
worthwhile form of expression, if they are to remain
creative and healthy human beings.

The fact that adaptation will increasingly demand conscious efforts need not imply a tragic view of life. Indeed, the necessity to respond vigorously to the environment, and the efforts involved in mastering oneself, as
well as in learning, are precisely the elements that give
structure and meaning to life. For, in final analysis, the
potentialities of human beings become actualized into the
form of a living reality only through the process of meet-
ing challenges in a creative spirit. History teaches that
man without effort is sure to deteriorate; man cannot
progress without effort, and man cannot be happy without effort.

THE GROWTH OF MANKIND

Self-satisfied Societies

THE HUMAN FUTURE is not what is inevitably bound to happen, a situation determined by antecedent events and by the blind operation of natural forces. What happens to man, and to the environment in which he lives, is conditioned to a large extent by human imagination and human will.

As judged from history, the most common human desire under normal circumstances has been to improve what already existed rather than to set on a new course. In other words, men usually try to make the future resemble the present as closely as possible. Often in the past this attitude has slowed down social evolution, resulting in the existence of what Arnold Toynbee has called "arrested societies." The Polynesian Islanders and the Eskimoes, for example, had arrived many centuries ago at a formula of existence admirably suited to the physical and economic conditions of their particular environment; their ancestral ways of life provided the kind of comfort and the satisfactions that come from carrying out, effectively and esthetically, the functions required for group survival. However, maintenance of the social *status quo* through the teaching and practices of traditions is no longer possible in modern times, not even for remote,

112

isolated people. All "arrested societies" are rapidly dis-integrating or at least are being profoundly transformed, as a result of the enormous increase in means of communication. They die or they must evolve when they come into contact with aggressor populations or with more competitive cultures.

Everywhere, now, progress has become the watchword. Progress, however, means only forward motion, not necessarily change for the better, nor even transformation in the ways of life. In fact, the predominant attitude in much of the Western world, and perhaps especially in the United States, is to substitute for the desire to maintain the traditional state of affairs, which is characteristic of static societies, another desire which is not fundamentally different. It consists in planning the future so as to maintain the same kind of life, only with more of everything and with perfected mechanical operations.

The willingness to accept change as a matter of course became very early a trademark of life in the United States. The French sociologist Alexis de Tocqueville emphasized this as one of the typical American traits in his *Democracy in America,* published in 1839: "I accost an American sailor and inquire why the ships of his country are built so as to last but for a short time; he answers . . . that the art of navigation is everyday making such progress, that the finest vessel would become almost useless if it lasted beyond a few years. In these words, which fell accidentally . . . from an uninstructed man, I recognized the general and systematic idea upon which a great people direct all their concerns." With his usual perspicacity, De Tocqueville recognized that this attitude was the extension of a general faith in the endless perfectibility of man, which the Western world, and especially America, had adopted enthusiastically from the Enlightenment philosophers. With time, however, the concept of perfectibility and of progress has deteriorated. There is still belief in progress, but, in general, this refers now to mechanical convenience and to an increase in quantity of goods rather than to real qualitative changes in human life.

One cannot contemplate without bewilderment, and even anguish, the frantic efforts of Western civilization to produce more and more of what is already produces, in overwhelming and, at times, nauseating amounts—whether it be mechanical contrivances or miracle drugs, specialized athletes or bathing beauties, copy writers or Ph.D.'s who despite their title are contemptuous of philosophy. The exclusive emphasis on mass production calls to mind the swarmings of locusts or of lemmings, which seem for a time such irresistible forces of nature, until, suddenly, they end in a disaster—the so-called population crashes.

Modern technology provides us with great efficiency for the mechanics of living. But while the evolution of the modern world makes it better adapted to a technological way of life, our kind of progress also condemns us to live within the narrow confines of this specific type of civilization. It might be well to remember in this respect that perfect fitness to a narrow range of environmental conditions is often the prelude to biological decadence and to extinction. The dinosaurs ruled over the Mesozoic world, but they disappeared when conditions began to change. In contrast, less specialized creatures survived, because their very lack of specialization made it possible for them to evolve.

To the extent that we want only more of what we already have, we are in the process of becoming a self-satisfied society without vital thoughts of renewal. Gilding of the lily is the modern counterpart of the social stagnation which characterized arrested societies in the past. If tomorrow is to be in all essentials like today, the lassitude that comes from advancing, for all time to come, on the same road will probably spell, in the long run, the extinction of our societies. Ortega y Gasset pointed out, in *The Revolt of the Masses,* that "our famous plentitude is in reality a coming to an end. There are centuries which die of self-satisfaction through not knowing how to renew their desires."

Stability, comfort, and even high refinements, are not enough to nourish human nature; the body survives but the spirit loses its vitality unless stimulated by new models created by imagination. Working out solutions for problems which have no transcendental meaning soon becomes boring. To keep really alive, men must raise their sights to some high purpose, best perhaps to one divorced from the satisfactions of animal appetites. Human life, like all other forms of life, is not concerned only with perpetuating itself and satisfying itself. It must surpass itself; otherwise it becomes just a waiting for death.

The Cross Principle

HUMAN INSTITUTIONS and civilizations die, but mankind survives and continues moving forward and upward. It continues moving because human beings are more resilient than the institutions of which they are a part, and especially because some remain creative, even though their civilization has exhausted its collective potentialities. More important, perhaps, there have always been men willing to struggle, to suffer and even to die for causes unrelated to their own interest or comfort.

The climax of the evolutionary process which has raised inanimate matter, first to the level of organic life, and then to conscious human thought, is the effort to create a new kind of human life through civilization. It is not yet possible to identify the leaders who are today shaping human destiny and will give historical glamor to our times. But there immediately come to mind many heroic figures of the past who chose self-sacrifice as if

they knew in the marrow of their bones, probably more
than by intellectual understanding, that unless the grain
dies, it bears no fruit.

Despite the selfishness of each individual human being,
mankind at large has some deep belief in the symbolic
significance of sacrifice—as shown by the fact that there
exists a sort of universal Golden Book of posterity on
which are written the names of martyrs to noble causes.
Generation after generation, schoolchildren learn the
words that Leonidas carved on the walls of the Ther-
mopyles: "Passerby, go and tell Sparta that here three
hundred Greeks died to obey her laws." Books are still
being written to memorialize the fact that Socrates re-
fused the chance to escape death, because he regarded
his ethical integrity and the respect of the laws of Athens
as more important than his very life. A short question
that Leonardo da Vinci scribbled in one of his notebooks
has been quoted time and time again. "Leonardo, *perchè
tanto peni?*" (Why do you take so much trouble for your
work?) Leonardo may not have been able to formulate
the answer to his own question, yet, to the end of his
days, he strove not only for esthetic perfection but also
for scientific knowledge, even though most of his efforts
remained unnoticed during his lifetime and acquired full
significance only after his death. Implicitly, Leonardo's
question symbolizes faith in the transcendental value of
human effort.

Condorcet's views on the inevitability of progress, quoted
earlier, acquire special significance from the fact that he
wrote them while under the threat of impending death,
knowing that he was doomed by his political convictions.
He expressed an optimistic view of the human fate, even
though his own days were numbered, and he would never
see the ideal world he envisaged. Likewise, the signers of
the Declaration of Independence proclaimed that the pursuit of happiness is an inalienable right of man, but they

were willing to struggle, to risk discomfort, and even to die for the defense of this belief. What they emphasized was not happiness *per se,* but the freedom for every man to pursue happiness by moving toward goals and by struggling for ideals of his own choice.

Thus human actions are determined by a causality which is not that of blind nature. This causality must be engendered by free volition, unless one assumes that there exists in man a peculiar kind of natural force which compels him to accept a share of efforts in the common works of mankind. Such an innate moral necessity was indeed suggested by Marcel Proust when he wrote in *Remembrance of Things Past*—on the day before he died —of those obligations which compel the artist to painful efforts amounting to self-sacrifice. These obligations, Proust wrote, appear to be derived from some world other than that of everyday material life, "based on goodness, scrupulousness, sacrifice . . . laws to which we are brought by every profound exercise of the intelligence."

Self-sacrifice occurs, of course, among animals, especially for the protection of the young. Indeed, some form of altruism runs like a thread deeply woven in the very fabric of living creation. The geneticist Sewall Wright went as far as suggesting the existence of what he called "altruistic genes" which would have survival value for the populations in which they occur. It is in man, however, that altruistic tendencies have become the most widespread and reach their highest form, to the extent of becoming a fundamental aspect of social behavior. Their importance is symbolized by "The Cross Principle" of Christianity. Altruism may cost the lives of those who practice it, yet it is accepted—in theory, at least—as a law of life by all civilized people. One of the most extraordinary paradoxes of human nature is that for millennia all civilizations have regarded sacrifice, in one form or another, as contributing to the furtherance of life.

Husbanding Human Wealth

FEW OF US, of course, are capable of de-
voting all our energies, let alone of sacrificing our lives,
to causes that transcend our personal interests. But all of
us can cultivate the awareness that we do not function
as self-sufficient entities, that we are part of a continuous
creative effort which is making mankind. Seen in this
light, human activities acquire a meaning and have consequences which go beyond their present effects; they
must be evaluated from the point of view of their long-
range influence on the total human enterprise. The least
we can do is to leave for those who will follow us a
world as good as that which we have inherited from the
past. The ultimate symbol of irresponsibility and of decadence are the words attributed to Louis XV: *"Après moi,
le déluge."*

Among the obvious responsibilities toward the future
are those concerning the preservation of natural resources. Much of our present prosperity comes from the
exploitation of mineral and plant wealth, which has accumulated on the globe through the slow processes of nature, and which cannot readily be replenished after it has
been exhausted. There is a great likelihood that even
water will be among the many commodities that will become scarce in a not too distant future. The water table
is falling rapidly in all populated areas; large cities must
bring water from hundreds of miles at ever increasing
costs, and the need for it continues to increase. Yet sheer
wastage goes on, without any concern for the future, as
illustrated by recent irrigation programs in Arizona. Some
twenty years ago, there was discovered in Arizona a large
reservoir of so-called fossil water. This water is designated "fossil" because it was trapped during the last Ice
Age and preserved at great depth underground ever since.

Although abundant, the supply of fossil water is limited; furthermore, it will not be replenished, once exhausted. Yet the fossil water is being pumped up to irrigate new fashionable golf courses, on the surface of which it is rapidly and irredeemably lost by evaporation. Of minor importance by itself, the waste of fossil water in Arizona constitutes a symbol of the waste of natural resources which are unreplenishable and are used for selfish ends, without concern for the future.

As an excuse for the thoughtless destruction of the natural resources which have accumulated in the course of time, it is commonly said that the loss is of no consequence, because science will eventually provide new materials and new sources of power to take their place. In reality, however, it is unjustified to believe that the possibilities of technological development are unlimited. Modern technology is geared to abundant supplies of cheap raw materials, and costs of production are therefore likely to increase, when certain of these materials become scarce. The technological triumphs of the past provide no assurance of what can be done in the future, because they were based on an abundant supply of natural resources in a conveniently available state.

Technology is based on theoretical scientific knowledge and this in turn is a commodity that we have inherited from the past. Theoretical science must be continually added to, for the sake both of understanding the universe and of continued technological growth. This sense of the continuity of knowledge is not new. In fact, it was clearly expressed by Denis Diderot in the introduction to his great Encyclopedia. "The purpose of an Encyclopedia," Diderot wrote, "is to assemble the knowledge scattered over the surface of the Earth; and to transmit it to the men who come after us; in order that the labors of centuries past may not be in vain during the centuries to come; that our descendants, by becoming better instructed, may as a consequence be more virtuous and happier, and that we may not die without having deserved well of the human race."

In contrast to Diderot's words, it is rather distressing to note how the general public today, as well as many persons in high position, insist that all learning be directed to immediate practical ends. It is true, of course, that our present prosperity results in large part from scientific research pointed to very practical questions. But it is also a fact that the very processes of modern thinking, and the fundamental basis on which all modern science is erected, have their origin in the abstract speculations of Greek philosophers and in the theoretical studies of the seventeenth-, eighteenth-, and nineteenth-century theoretical scientists.

The background of knowledge on which we depend was created by dedicated men who searched the laws of reason and of nature, even though their discoveries contributed nothing to their own welfare or to the economic structure of their times. Without this basis, slowly built over many centuries, modern culture and technology would not exist. To the extent that we exploit the intellectual wealth inherited from the past, without making the effort to accumulate theoretical knowledge not of practical use to us, we act as selfish tenants who exhaust and destroy the land of their ancestors and prepare the intellectual dust bowls of the future.

The fact never to be forgotten is that we are the beneficiaries of the wealth and wisdom that our ancestors acquired through centuries of painful effort. Most of the splendors of our civilization are not of our own making; we are enjoying a heritage rich in material goods, in experience, and in knowledge.

All of us, for example, have derived pleasure and inspiration from the architectural monuments that have survived from the past. Above and beyond their esthetic value these monuments symbolize the historical continuity of mankind—the fact that human existence transcends the life of each particular individual. How much the world would lose of its human appeal, emotional and esthetic, if it were deprived of the venerable structures that men have left as witnesses of their passage—the Celtic dolmens and the Greeek temples; the Tibetan monasteries and the Gothic cathedrals; the Roman aqueducts and the Renaissance palaces; the great public monuments and memorials to heroes. By the same token, should we not give thought to what our own civilization will leave for the generations to come? Where are the monuments of today that will still be standing two thousand years hence? Where are the gardens, parks, and avenues of trees made of lasting species and planted in a noble style, that could become increasingly poetical and majestic with added centuries?

Even the charm of our countryside must not be taken for granted, as if it were a gift of nature. Only two kinds of landscape are fully satisfying. One is primeval nature undisturbed by man—of which we shall have less and less, as the world population increases. The other kind of landscape is one in which man has toiled for generations, creating through centuries of patient trial and error a kind of harmony between himself and the physical environment. Wherever man has lived and worked, forests have been disciplined; swamps have been drained; the banks of rivers have been contained; roads have been opened; rocks and roots have been cleared to create the fertile ground of fields and of gardens.

What we long for and find in the country is not nature in the raw; it is an atmosphere suited to human needs, determined by physiological and emotional aspirations engendered by millennia of civilized life. The appealing human quality of woodland and of farming country is not inherent in nature. It is the very human creation of our ancestors who toiled to shape intractable forest, land, and water into a pattern suitable for mankind. This quality will not long survive if preoccupations with real estate projects, factory sites, and concrete highways become the exclusive determinants of land planning.

Modern man may state, of course, that the genius of our culture is not to create lasting monuments but rather to erect utilitarian buildings as they are required, then tear them down when something else becomes more practical or economical. The danger in this attitude is that planned obsolescence is not only a technological philosophy; it implies also a fundamental assumption about the human world. The implication is that only the present counts, that the past might just as well be forgotten, except to be exploited, and that the future will have to take care of itself. In the long run, this attitude is likely to render existence meaningless and to dull vision, because there is no perspective without retrospection. It will engender a society dedicated to nothing beyond techniques and mechanical pleasures, without any awareness of the historical and emotional significance of the human condition.

It is perhaps true, although it has not been proved, that planned obsolescence is justified economically with regard to dwellings, factories, offices, or amusement grounds. But to build nothing capable of surviving our times is a sign of irresponsibility toward our descendants, a failure to do for them what the men of the past have done for us; in brief, a refusal to continue the tradition which has carried mankind beyond its brutish origins. In contrast, to create for the future is not only a duty but also a source of deep satisfaction for the human mind, a gesture that gives significance even to the most trivial tasks.

To work merely for the present constitutes, from all points of view, a betrayal of human obligations. It cor-

responds to the denial of an attitude which is associated with the greatest achievements of mankind, namely,
the willingness to struggle and even to die for a transcendental cause. The most fundamental aspect of the human
condition is that individual life cannot be considered as
an end unto itself. In one form or another, all worthy men,
whether they be pagans or Christians, mystics or atheists,
have searched for a justification of their existence in tasks
from which they could not hope to derive any earthly
profit. Individual men cannot find their fulfillment except
in mankind.

Growth and Decay of Civilizations

ACCORDING TO the French proverb, *"Les
gens heureux n'ont pas d'histoire."* But while it may be
true that the periods of happiness are the blank pages of
history, it is also a fact that most happy persons conceal
behind their contented public self another self which is
unfulfilled and yearns to make history. Like Alphonse
Daudet's *Tartarin de Tarascon,* we dream of hunting big
game in Africa even while calling for a cup of hot choco-
late in bed. In each one of us there coexists a Don Quixote eager to fight for a fair lady who exists only in our
imagination, and a Sancho Panza who would much rather
settle down and enjoy peacefully the fruits of the earth.
Sancho Panza is the realistic man, but, in fact, it is the
unpractical Don Quixote who keeps mankind on the
move. Moreover, his dreams come to life as by a mi-
raculous act of creation, thereby enriching and bright-
ening all of human experience.

Like Don Quixote's Dulcinea, civilizations are strange
immaterial beings which acquire a life of their own, after
emerging from the minds of dreamers. Twenty-five hundred years ago, a few argumentative Greeks launched a

sophisticated, rational way of thinking which seemed to have no chance of survival among the irrational barbarians of Europe. Yet, the rational attitude lived on, eventually converting the Western world to the Greco-Roman culture. Early in the Middle Ages, some ascetic monks and roving troubadours taught the cult of the Virgin Mary to the quarrelsome barons and the crude peasants of Northern France, and, as a result, ethereal chapels and cathedrals with their colored windows emerged from the rough medieval world. In the seventeenth century, a handful of men intoxicated with the love of abstract knowledge created experimental science; and out of this intellectual game there grew the Industrial Revolution and, eventually, the Manhattan skyline. The creations of man thus behave as if they moved on by a force of their own, once they have escaped from the minds of their creators. Indeed, they usually move rapidly and reach beyond what was expected of them. But they are unpredictable creatures and can become dangerous; their collapse can bury mankind under rubble.

Civilizations commonly become intoxicated with their technological proficiency. The architects of the late Gothic style had such confidence in their skill, that they built higher and higher structures with more and more flamboyant ogives; and, as a result, the high towers collapsed, as in Beauvais, leaving on the ground immense soulless bodies. It does not take much imagination to see in these architectural catastrophes a symbol of what might be in store for our civilization. But even though the modern world can escape catastrophic destruction, there exist dangers to the well-being of the social body which are inherent in undisciplined technological growth. We are already suffering from the problems posed by crowding, by air pollution, by automobile traffic, and by countless products of industrial life. And the social disturbances that are likely to result from automation are so apparent that they have begun to preoccupy social conscience even before they have occurred on a significant scale.

Norbert Wiener, who became one of the prophets of the automation age through his book *Cybernetics,* seems to take a sardonic pleasure in emphasizing that symbolic forecasts of the dangers attendant to the use of mechanical brains can be found in several ancient legends. In the Arabian Nights' Entertainments, the genie in the bottle, once released by the fisherman, has a destructive will of its own. The Sorcerer's Apprentice learns the words by which the broomstick is made to fetch water but does not know the words to stop it. In W. W. Jacobs' story, the owner of the enchanted monkey's paw gets a small fortune at the cost of mangling his son in the machinery of the factory in which he works. "There is nothing which will automatically make the automatic factory work for human good," writes Norbert Wiener, "unless we have determined this human good in advance and have so constructed the factory as to contribute to it." Thus, automation, like other new technological developments, creates new problems of social ethics with responsibilities which are profound because they concern so many lives, yet almost impersonal because they involve the play of anonymous and blind natural forces.

Curiously enough, the very efficiency of our technological civilization may be one of its undoings. Through specialization in knowledge, in management, and in technical skills, our society has succeeded in producing an extraordinary state of adaptedness between human life and the environment that it creates. But this adaptedness and the efficiency which it makes possible impose severe limitations on the freedom to change. These limitations imply a fundamental conservatism which substitutes endless play with trivial details for significantly progressive changes. The history of living things shows that, in general, the more specialized and efficient forms find it diffi-

cult to undergo adaptive modifications when placed in a
new environment; and there are indications that, for
human societies as well, adaptability decreases with increasing specialization. Overspecialized and overadapted
cultures, like that of the United States of America, might
find it difficult, for example, to move on to the next phase
of human evolution, to get over the divide which separates
present-day industrial civilization from a more sophisticated social and cultural way of life.

It is perhaps for this reason that civilizations commonly
lose the will or the ability to change, after they have set
on a certain course. The general pattern is that each particular civilization soon exhausts the spiritual content and
creativeness which characterized its initial phase; then,
for a period, it retains a certain kind of vigor based on
orthodox classicism; and, finally, it degenerates into
triviality.

Historians and philosophers have pointed out that our
age presents, in this regard, many similarities to the Hellenistic era which lingered on for several centuries, after
the great outburst of enthusiasm and genius which gave
birth to the Hellenic culture. Like our own age, and in
contrast to the short period of great Hellenic culture, the
Hellenistic era was characterized by enormous cities,
highly organized commercial developments, bizarre forms
of art, emphasis on specialized knowledge. There were
great libraries and centers of learning, but freshness had
gradually vanished; the ardor for intellectual adventure
had been replaced by orthodox culture and by learned
taste. Similarly, the official standard-bearers of our culture are more likely to be the champions of traditional
learning than the boldly original spirits willing to venture
on untrodden intellectual and spiritual paths.

History teaches that orthodox intellectualism can continue to prosper for a long time after its cultural climax—
as do most orthodoxies. In the end, however, orthodoxy

withers from lack of an inner creative urge, and, eventually, it yields to less refined but more vigorous faiths. Hellenistic civilization yielded to Christian culture after it had lost the Hellenic inspiration and had become academic. Similarly, the great medieval civilization became scholastic and then had to yield to scientific rationalism and to the philosophy of the Enlightenment. And now there are indications that our own era is losing faith in the spiritual values which gave rise to Western culture. Western civilization still moves mightily under the momentum of scientific materialism, but it does not succeed in defining the good life. It is all dressed up with no place to go.

What is most disturbing, perhaps, is the tendency to take for granted, as a natural birthright, blessings which are ours only through the efforts of those who came before us. Modern mass man assumes that the social and technical structure, which he has inherited from his ancestors, has been produced by nature; he does not realize that the creation of this new world demanded the painful efforts of highly endowed individuals. Still less does he recognize that civilization cannot long survive without the practice of certain difficult human virtues. While it is natural and desirable that modern man should be intensely concerned with his well-being, this is not a sufficient motivation to keep modern culture alive for very long. Even a cursory observation of our society reveals obvious symptoms of disintegration, owing to the lack of a unifying faith of purpose.

There are, of course, the beatniks and the angry young men, adrift in a society that they despise; but there are also the hardworking and creative scholars and artists who withdraw from society for the same reason. There are the gangsters and narcotic peddlers; but, more importantly, there are the countless businessmen and technologists who labor furiously to mass-produce and to promote industrial goods in which they themselves do not believe, even though they know that these goods are not needed and can even be dangerous. There is the widespread awareness of decadence and ugliness in our great urban areas, the breakdown in public means of transportation, the overwhelming accent on gross materialistic and selfish comfort, the absence of personal and social discipline, the sacrifice of quality to quantity in production as well as in education. The most discouraging aspect of the lack of creative response to these threats is that, although all thinking persons are aware of the situation and at heart are anxious to do something to correct it, common action cannot be mustered, because it would demand a common faith that does not exist.

The Faith in the Human Fate

THE CYNICS, or those who consider themselves realists, can in fairness point out that searching for a new faith that would unite society is like chasing a will-o'-the-wisp. Many kinds of philosophical, social, and religious faiths have appeared in the course of history, only to disappear like shooting stars consuming themselves in the sky. The Greeks launched Western culture on its course with an ideal of perfection which has never been surpassed, but very soon Greek art forms became lifeless and repetitious, Greek philosophy became hairsplitting and barren formulae, Greek science an endless elaboration of details based on unquestioned premises. Christianity was at first pure love, then mystical genius, during the thirteenth century; but now it often degenerates into conservative and uninspired social ethics. Scientific rationalism had promised to explain the riddle of the world, but today the most sophisticated scientists recognize and emphasize the inherent limitations of human knowledge and of scientific understanding. What remains at the most is a sort

of childish confidence that science can solve all technological problems—and even this confidence has been tar-
nished by the increasing awareness that power and wealth
do not necessarily make for a happy life.

Why, then, speak of national purpose, social purpose,
or any kind of purpose? In reality, no one can tell where
the goals are, not even define what is the good life that
mankind should try to achieve. It seems that the difficulty
here might reside in the fact that we are asking the wrong
questions, and misinterpreting history. The Greeks of the
Hellenic period did not live for a precise purpose, or work
toward a common goal; neither did the builders of cathedrals or the founders of scientific rationalism. Instead,
what characterized the creators of great civilizations was
that they believed in a set of values which transcended
comfort, effortless existence, and the pleasure of the moment; their faith was not an abstract *Faith* but a sort of
emotional trust in the human condition. They also had the
will to plan for the future and to live according to these
values. We, too, make judgments of values. In fact, these
values are the most compelling determinants of our individual lives. And it is in this respect that human evolution
continues to differ so profoundly from ordinary biological
evolution.

In plants and animals under natural circumstances,
biological success is determined by the ability to survive
and to multiply. The biological study of any kind of
organism involves questions, such as, "When and where
did it first appear? What has been its evolution? What is
its structure? What are the mechanisms of its physicochemical processes?" All these questions are as valid for
man as for other living things. But they leave out of consideration the problems which are most important for
human life. It would be good to know more of the origin
of life, of its development, and of its present state, but
the peculiar concern of man is the future—indeed, some

kind of immortality. Curiously enough, it need not be a
precise image of the future, only a vision on some open
vista with a promise of ascending growth toward a better
world. As I write these lines two contrasting pictures
come to my mind, one of a juvenile delinquent, the other
of a painting by Daumier.

The fundamental characteristic of the true juvenile delinquent is that he acts only for the sake of the present,
for the satisfaction of an urge, of an appetite, or of a
whim. He has not learned that man differs from animals
by consciously relating the present to the future; indeed,
he has no vision whatever of the future. In contrast, the
masterpiece by Daumier, *The Uprising,* seems to be a
symbol of human willingness to struggle for the future.
This painting, in the Phillips Gallery in Washington, shows
a vigorous and handsome young man on a barricade with
outstretched arms and clenched fists. His visionary gaze
is lost in the distance toward a future that he will never
know, because he will not live long enough; bullets will
probably soon strike him down. Certainly it is a vague
future that the revolutionary on the barricade sees in his
imagination; at most it means Liberty, perhaps Equality
and Fraternity. But Daumier's hero is the symbol of *Man,*
the animal with an open future which he creates through
faith in the human condition. He is the eternal nomad of
the questioning spirit, haunted by the future and blind
to danger, the eternal standard-bearer of a worthwhile
cause.

Like the classical Greeks, like the cathedral builders,
like the rationalists, and like Daumier's revolutionary on
the barricade, modern man also has made judgments of
values. He knows that it is important to accept sacrifices
for the defense of one's homeland and for worthwhile
ideals; to help one's fellow man in need; to work toward
improving one's community; to advance knowledge even
without hope of financial rewards; to enlarge and enrich

the intellectual and emotional perception of the cosmos through science, literature, and the arts. He realizes more and more the truth preached by philosophers for several millennia, that the selfish pursuit of happiness always ends in disappointment.

The awareness that individual human lives acquire value and meaning only when they transcend themselves has taken many different forms. It can be a disenchanted challenge to fate, as when Thomas Wolfe wrote in *You Can't Go Home Again,* "Man was born to live, to suffer and to die, and what befalls him is a tragic lot. There is no denying this in the final end. But we must deny it all along the way." It can be Sören Kierkegaard's call to action, when he wrote, "To venture causes anxiety. But not to venture is to lose oneself." Or it can be the belief expressed by Albert Camus, that while he who trusts in the human fate may be a fool, he who despairs of events is a coward. Whichever way it is expressed, the view that man can transcend his selfish interests, even for forlorn causes, is the mark of a profound and creative faith in the human condition.

The fundamental human value is the freedom to choose, and, if need be, to elect painful effort, dangerous risks, and responsibilities for the sake of some transcendental value. It is this way of life which differentiates man from the rest of creation. It corresponds to a faith more entrancing and more comprehensive than the view of the good life by the Greek philosophers, than the vision of heaven by the Medievalists, than the mathematical world conceived by the rational scientists, than the utopian societies imagined by political reformers. It is the largest possible faith, simply because it is open on an endless future with unlimited possibilities.

The symbolic representation of this open future is everywhere. The scientist finds it in the theory of cosmic evolution, with the gradual insertion of more and more

freedom into matter; the sociologist, in the endless creation of new utopias describing perfect imaginary states
that men try to convert into reality; the artist, in the creation of a visionary world that transcends his selfish interest. The ultimate expression of the open future is William
Blake's urging that we "learn to apprehend the world with
unobstructed senses" because, in his words, "if the doors
of perception were cleansed, everything would appear to
man as it is, infinite."

The Nonmaterial Facts of Human Life

DESPITE so many setbacks in the intellec-
tual and ethical growth of man; despite so much evidence
that his innate endowments are often spoiled by material
civilization; despite the folly, triviality, vulgarity, and
cruelty which taint most of his motives and actions, nevertheless there is reassuring evidence that mankind does
become better, even though the improvement is so dis-
couragingly slow and erratic. Slavery was taken as a matter
of course one thousand years ago. Today it is still practiced in one form or another, but it is no longer acceptable to the collective conscience of modern man. While
there is so much reason to despair, yet it is part of the
human duty to believe that mankind can continue to move
forward and upward.

As far as we can judge, man differs from the rest of
creation by his wider range of freedom and by the greater
extent to which he can, and does, exercise free will. Not
only does he have a large degree of latitude in his decision
to act or not to act, but, more importantly, he is often
aware of the reasons that make him select the cause to
which he dedicates his action. Free will, however, implies
choice and a motive; and motive is a matter of faith. In
final analysis, choice is rarely possible without some vision

of the future. In fact, it is the possibility, nay, the inescapable need to choose, which gives its grandeur to the human condition, and which also accounts for its tragic quality.

In most cases, the choice that must be made is not between alternatives to be experienced personally and in the present; it is between courses of action which affect other human beings and which involve the future. For a cat, the decision to move nearer the stove or toward a sunny window may involve, chiefly, the perception of a more pleasant temperature. But for man, almost any kind of decision is likely to involve something more than his comfort; he must think of his neighbors, and he must consider the advisability of forgoing the pleasure of the moment for the sake of the morrow.

The need to choose is, perhaps, the most constant aspect of conscious human life; it constitutes both its greatest asset and its heaviest burden. In every person, now and then, and in most persons, very frequently, there arises the desire to escape the responsibility of having to make decisions which engage not only the self, but also one's fellow men and the future. In its crudest expression, this intellectual and emotional weariness takes the form of a longing to achieve the peace of mind symbolized by the passive gaze of the contented cow. In a more sophisticated manner, the same wish comes forth in the words that Thoreau wrote for his journal while drifting idly on Walden pond, and letting himself become a part of his surroundings, as if he were a completely passive creature. He thought then that man could be so much happier "just being" rather than "living." Like Thoreau on Walden pond, or a cat basking in the sun, man can indeed enjoy "just being," but usually he cannot bear the enjoyment for very long. Whatever the hardships and the efforts that living entails, men want to live, not just to be. Consciously or unconsciously, most of them take the attitude expressed by Secondhorn in Bernard Shaw's *Buoyant Billions:* "I don't want to be happy; I want to be alive and active."

Despite their oft-repeated assertion that the ideal would be to "return to nature" so as to recapture simple physical contentment, human beings are not long satisfied with a form of happiness based on such a passive philosophy. Their ultimate reaction is to escape from paradise and to search for adventure, even if this means struggle and sufferings. Such was the case for Herman Melville when he decided to leave the Polynesian island of Typee. Melville had spent six happy months among the Typees who had welcomed him in their idyllic valley after his shipwreck. He was enchanted by their "continued happiness . . . the mere buoyant sense of a healthful physical existence," and he admired the lack of competitive spirit in their society. Yet he could not long endure their passive happiness; he actually risked death in order to escape from his Polynesian paradise and to return to the physical and mental misery of his life in New England.

D. H. Lawrence also suffered acutely from the manner of living imposed by the Industrial Civilization, and he believed that we should "destroy our false, inorganic connexions . . . and re-establish the living connexions, with the cosmos, the sun and earth." Yet while he urged his fellow Europeans to recover the direct primary sensations of unadulterated life, he came to despise the manifestations of simple, animal contentment on the face of a people who were close to these primeval virtues. The timeless, unworried expression of the Samoans made him realize that, for Western man, awareness of the past and preoccupation with the future have become essential ingredients of life.

Like many romantics, Nietzsche claimed that he envied the animals because they did not know the past, were not concerned with the future, and lived only in the present.

Hegel also stated that the periods of happiness are the "empty periods of history." In support of his statement is the fact that the pages of our era are filled to the brim, and that we are not particularly happy. But mankind will not go back; the moving force is not the search for happiness, but the desire to fill the pages of history.

Man exercises free will not only by conducting his life of the present for the sake of a future that he can barely imagine, but also by concerning himself with problems that have no obvious bearing on his selfish biological comfort and welfare. It is painfully obvious, of course, that cruelty based on selfishness still governs much of human action. Today as in the past, man is wolf to man. But it is equally true, and more interesting, that respect for life has become one of the tenets of philosophy in many cultures. It is a human ideal which extends in principle to all living forms—granted that it is often ignored in practice.

The skeptic does not lack arguments to defend the view that man is, after all, little more than an animal. In particular, he can point to the fact that the appetites of mankind are still much the same as they were before Paleolithic times. In prosperous refined cities, as well as in tropical forests or in arid deserts, the most common urge of the growing child is to eat as much and as often as possible; everywhere the dream of the young adult male is a woman all his own. But for mankind all over the world—including growing children and young adult males—food and sex and all instinctual hungers commonly take second place to emotions and adventures which are meaningless for animals. The universal appeal of Don Quixote's adventures for young, adult, and old alike is an expression of this "unnatural" aspect of human nature. Quixote embodies the peculiarly human willingness to risk danger and hardship for no better reason than achieving some feat memorable or noble. He is one of the great symbols of mankind because he stands for the desire to attempt the impossible for the sake of greatness without any hope of material reward.

Even in our times, which are said to be so materialistic and so scornful of ideals, what really excites the world is the account of a dramatic rescue at sea or in the bottom of a mine; of an idealist allowing himself to die of starvation for the sake of his country's political freedom; the struggles of an explorer reaching for the Pole or climbing Mount Everest; the daring of Lindbergh's first crossing of the Atlantic, or of astronauts shot into space. These events do not in any way affect the everyday life of the common man, nor have they any meaning that can be referred to the animal basis of mankind. But they bring to light two aspects of human nature which are more important than the traits that man has inherited from his animal past. One is the sense of belonging to a community—mankind—which, progressively, in the course of time, has come to encompass the whole world. The other is the sense of participation in a great adventure that transcends the search for the satisfaction of material needs and pleasures.

This unselfish manifestation of human nature is not new; in fact, it is as ancient as recorded history. In all cultures that we know of, there have been men who have shunned the abundant life and who have chosen instead asceticism, suffering, and otherworldliness. Some have been saints intoxicated with God, others have been very reasonable and otherwise ordinary persons obeying the dictates of their conscience. Socrates has become a legendary figure not so much by reason of his philosophy as by his willingness to accept death rather than violate the laws to which he owed the nature of his very self.

The spirit of human brotherhood and the urge to move forward and upward are not to be described in terms of chemical constitution and physical forces, but they are facts, nevertheless, just as real as the need for food, the love of comfort, or the fear of pain. As facts they differ from those of the so-called natural sciences, because they are concerned with consequences rather than being determined by antecedent causes. One could almost say that they are made not of matter, but of time and spirit because their chief constituents are memories of the past, anticipations of the future, and choice of values. But even though they arise from expectations, from visions of the mind, indeed from dreams, they are so real and powerful that they can sway human behavior and are thereby the most effective forces in changing the face of the earth. Thus it is certain that man cannot be completely understood merely by considering him as a piece of machinery to be dissected and analyzed objectively by the methods of the exact sciences. To be understood man must be "known" in the Biblical sense; he must be encountered and experienced as a dreaming and throbbing creature.

ENVOI

MORNING AND EVENING, summer and winter, walking back and forth from work, I give thanks to those who planted on the grounds of the Rockefeller Institute, more than half a century ago, the rows of sycamore trees which today look so noble against the background of New York City. Always also I have in mind the avenues of venerable trees along the roads of France, and in the parks where I played as a child. This is why I now plant and tend a few trees every year. I shall not live long enough to see them reach full size; nevertheless, I perceive them in all their glory with that marvelous sense organ which is peculiar to man, the imaginary vision of things to come. One finds in libraries a few books by the great landscape architects of the eighteenth century, showing drawings of the European parks at the time of their creation, and then a century later when the plantations had reached maturity. It is obvious that the landscape architects had composed the surfaces of water, of lawns and flowers to fit the silhouettes of trees and the masses of shrubbery not as they existed at the time, but as they were to become. And because landscape architects visualized the future and planned for it several centuries ago, millions of human beings enjoy today the great European parks and the classical gardens.

Throughout my life I have associated with men of the past who have written books and have transmitted to me their thoughts, their feelings, and the atmosphere of their age. The words of Socrates taking poison in order to remain true to his ethical faith always make me proud of belonging to mankind. For different but related reasons, my understanding and love of Paris has increased since reading in Jean Giraudoux that, looking at the city from the top of the Eiffel Tower, he could see the few square miles of human history where men have, in the course of time, the most thought, the most written, the most loved, and the most suffered. I, too, have written a few books, not with the illusion that they will be widely read, or alter the course of events, but with the hope of transmitting to some of my fellow men what I have received from so many others. I enjoy the thought of participating in the conversation which men have been carrying on from one land to the other across the centuries. It is this conversation which makes us what we are and helps each of us share in what all the others have experienced.

The story told of the three medieval hod carriers, toiling with their loads on the road leading to Chartres, symbolizes the significance of the part—small as it may be—that each one of us plays in the great human adventure: "What are you up to?" a passer-by asked them. "I am carting stones," one of the laborers answered. "I am working on a wall," said another. And the third replied, "I am building a cathedral." It may be drudgery to pull heavy stones and often dull to work on the construction of a wall, but the effort takes a new significance if it serves to build a cathedral—even though the laborer will not live long enough to see the monument completed. This is not an original nor a new philosophy. In fact, it corresponds to one of the most ancient and venerable human attitudes—the mysterious sense of responsibility toward the future, which has made so many men willing to work for causes that transcend their selfish interests. Concern for the future is the mark and the glory of the human condition. Men come and go, but however limited their individual strength, small their contribution, and short their life span, their efforts are never in vain because, like runners in a race, they hand on the torch of life.